Praise

'If you fear your present
unstructured and leave audiences underwhelmed,
this book is full of practical advice and real-life
examples to kickstart your journey to becoming a
confident and engaging communicator. Andrea has
broken the challenges of presenting into beautifully
bite-sized strategies, tools and insights to help you
devise and deliver presentations that truly serve
your audience and show you at your best.'
— **Rachel Schofield**, Career Coach and former
BBC presenter

'Having the keys to communicate your ideas
effectively will unlock huge opportunities. Problem
is, great ideas often fail, not because of the idea itself,
but because of how they're communicated. That's
a tragedy! Thankfully, Andrea wrote a book to save
the day. So do yourself (and your audience) a favour
– if you want to become the best presenter you can
be, read this book. It's the ultimate roadmap to what
makes a memorable presentation. It's the book I wish
I had read six years ago when I started my career as a
professional keynote speaker.'
— **Mark Leruste**, bestselling author of *Glow
in the Dark* and award-winning host of
The Unconventionalists podcast

'During my 32-year career at the World Bank Group,
I learned how to become a strong speaker the hard
way: experiencing what worked and what didn't.

I wish we had a book like this at the time. Andrea Pacini offers a deep dive into the art of creating compelling presentations and establishing strong connections with the audience. *Confident Presenter* gives you a practical process that everyone who works in the field should follow. As a bonus, it includes fascinating stories and examples. A great read indeed.'
— **Angelica Silvero**, Head, World Bank Group Speakers Bureau

'I always tell my clients and students that, when presenting, we need to focus on three Es: Educate, Engage and Excite. That's exactly what presentation expert Andrea Pacini does in his terrific new book! He provides a wealth of valuable content, captures and holds our attention from start to finish, and inspires us to want to put these ideas into practice. Filled with timeless tools, tips and techniques, *Confident Presenter* will help every reader to deliver their messages with greater poise, presence, and power ... so as to become a more competent, compelling and confident public speaker.'
— **Todd Cherches**, CEO of BigBlueGumball, adjunct Professor of Leadership at NYU and Columbia University and author of *VisuaLeadership: Leveraging the Power of Visual Thinking in Leadership and in Life*

'If I were still running a corporate team, this is a book I would give to every one of the managers in my team. It's mission critical advice, incredibly simply distilled. I appreciate how you can use it as a manual and reference after the first read. If any one of my previous brand managers had put even 20% of what Andrea teaches into practice, it would have made a massive impact on what they could achieve.'

— **Jessie Wölke**, Co-Founder of NO PLANET B

'It's an oddity of modern life that we admire others who are good public speakers, but we don't put in the hard yards to be good ourselves. However, good public speaking is a very attainable gift: all you need is a bit of effort and some intelligent guidance. The effort must come from you, but the guidance can come from this remarkable book. Andrea Pacini understands how presenting works (and how it sometimes doesn't) with real insight. Read it, study it, think about it and then enjoy the self-belief that comes with knowing how to present well.'

— **Roger Mavity**, author of *Life's a Pitch*, writer, business guru

'*Confident Presenter* is an indispensable guide for anyone who wants to create compelling presentations. The book's clear method gives you a set process for preparing presentations, making it easy to implement. If you are a business owner or leader who wants to create powerful presentations that will be remembered, appreciated and acted upon, you'll find this book to be an excellent resource. If you've ever wished you could create amazing presentations like the pros, *Confident Presenter* will show you how!'

— **Susanna Lawson**, Founder of OneFile

'Andrea Pacini is passionate about making people better presenters. In *Confident Presenter*, you feel that passion beginning on page one. What makes Pacini's book particularly valuable are the many example presentations upon which he anchors his lessons. Even more important than the successful examples, are the failures. Lessons borne of failure leave deeper impressions. Pacini's lessons are authentic – you can smell the blood.'

— **Michael Alley**, author of *The Craft of Scientific Presentations*

'I'm confident chatting to people casually, but in presentation mode it's suddenly difficult to make the impact I want. Not anymore – the content Andrea shares in this book has been a game changer for me. It's full of practical tools and examples you can relate to, ones which will help refine your skills so you can maximise the potential in your presentations. If you've ever felt overwhelmed by the process of creating and delivering a presentation, this book is an absolute must-read!'

— **Alan Furley**, Co-founder and CEO of ISL Talent

'In *Confident Presenter*, Andrea shares invaluable insights and techniques for captivating any audience. With a focus on practical advice and real-life examples, this book is a must-read for anyone looking to take their public speaking to the next level.'

— **Stephy Hogan**, Accessible Design Advocate at IBM and Co-founder of the Presentation Guild

'The structured approach set out in *Confident Presenter* is exciting – so many of the challenges that I've had over the years trying to create engaging presentations are directly tackled by Andrea. The framework that he sets out is so useful. I haven't seen anything like it before. It's super-powerful – as you work through each stage you build momentum, and confidence, so that you feel thrilled once you see the output.'

— **Colin Bryce**, Managing Director at Cobry

'A must-have in the armoury of anybody who does any form of presenting as part of their job. There's a huge difference between a PowerPoint and a successful presentation, and this book gets straight to the heart of it. Better yet, it's packed full of actionable and straightforward tips to take you to the next level. I read lots of business books and I cannot recommend this book more highly.'

— **Tom Katté**, Managing Director at Katté & Co

Confident Presenter

**INSPIRE YOUR AUDIENCE.
INCREASE YOUR INFLUENCE.
MAKE AN IMPACT.**

Andrea Pacini

R^ethink

First published in Great Britain in 2023 by Rethink Press (www.rethinkpress.com)

Cover image © Grant Wright

For Vale and Kian

Contents

Foreword

If you're in business, you need to lead, and if you aim to lead, you need people to follow you. Too many business managers feel that communication is something they do on a best-effort basis, in whatever available time they have, which usually ends up being not very much. If you've picked up this book, you already have some expectation that presentations should not be tortuous, so it might seem strange to you that many senior managers know nothing of their presentation until they get up to speak and discover their slides at the same time as their audience. This is not a recipe for success.

Over time, Ideas on Stage have distilled and honed the Presentation SCORE Method (or pSCORE for short). My colleague Andrea Pacini has applied pSCORE with great success in his role as Head of Ideas on Stage UK, helping many clients to stand out and shine. Like everyone in our team, Andrea is more than just a simple consultant able to reproduce a solid process: he has new ideas, new approaches and new ways to apply our methods.

This is what you will find in *Confident Presenter*. Andrea takes the five key success factors of pSCORE (Simple, Clear, Original, Related and Enjoyable) and shows you how to leverage them to produce high impact presentations and deliver them powerfully. Through many case studies and examples, Andrea brings pSCORE to life.

In my experience, around 80% of your comfort as a speaker comes from having clear objectives, knowing what you plan to say, and knowing that it is made to measure for your specific audience and has a good chance of hitting those objectives. If you want to be confident, this is key. Most of this book focuses, therefore, on crafting your storyline using simple ideas that any business professional can apply.

Confidence also stems from how you approach your presentation, how you prepare and how you speak. I like to think of storytelling as part story and part telling. Andrea also includes many practical tips to give you the best chance of feeling comfortable, speaking convincingly and becoming that Confident Presenter we all dream of being.

I've been living, breathing and teaching presentations for longer than I care to remember and I've read many excellent books on the subject. Of course, I'm a little biased in that Andrea is a colleague of mine and he's given me the honour of writing this Foreword, so you're welcome to take this with more than a pinch of salt if you wish, but for me *Confident Presenter* is a fine addition to any business bookshelf. It is far more than 'just another presentation book', and if you listen to Andrea and apply his wisdom, you'll be a big step closer to being the kind of leader people can't help following.

— **Phil Waknell**, Chief Inspiration Officer and Co-Founder, Ideas on Stage, Author, *Business Presentation Revolution: The Bold New Way to Inspire Action, Online or on Stage*

Introduction

Great ideas need wings. Too many great ideas have crashed and burned because they weren't presented well enough.

For example, a French professor had the bright idea that artificial intelligence could help to detect lung cancer at an early stage, but he was unable to convince the health authorities to fund his research. By a stroke of luck, he was asked to speak about his idea at a medical congress, whose organisers had asked Ideas on Stage to work with each speaker to make their talks less boring than usual. (Tip for most medical conventions: strong coffee.) A few weeks after the congress, the professor told us he had used the same presentation to pitch for funding again and had finally received the green light.

An idea needs wings, and that means a strong, well-delivered presentation.

Many business leaders believe that being confident at presenting comes naturally to some people. Perhaps they're born with confidence. Or they think that to become more confident at presenting, they simply need to improve their delivery skills and work on techniques like eye contact, body language and vocal delivery. These are all important, but there's so much more to it. Understanding your audience, having a clear objective, identifying your key messages, developing an engaging storyline – these steps are even more important than your delivery.

As a presentation coach and Head of Ideas on Stage UK, I specialise in working with business owners, leaders and their teams who want to become the best presenters in their industry. I'm so passionate about public speaking because, as a little kid growing up in Italy, I was surrounded by small business owners. My parents ran their own business trimming soles for shoes – a common industry in the region I come from. They still do. Growing up in that environment, I saw their challenges (raising four kids while trying to run a business isn't easy), but I also saw their spark, entrepreneurial mindset and proactive approach to life. That's why I always wanted to be an entrepreneur.

That remained a dream for a long time. Before doing what I'm doing now, I started many projects. All of them failed, but that's what helped me see that great ideas often fail not because of the idea itself, but because of how they're communicated. I launched a blog, but it didn't reach a massive audience because I didn't communicate it well enough. I created a newsletter with the idea of curating content for hundreds of thousands of people. I had less than 100 subscribers because I didn't communicate it well enough. I hosted a big event to raise money in support of underprivileged kids and it didn't make a massive impact because I didn't communicate it well enough.

That's why I started my own journey to learning communication and that's why I eventually became a presentation coach. That's why my life mission is to stop great ideas from failing just because of the way we present them. My mission is to help business owners, leaders and their teams become the best presenters they can be so they can grow their business and increase their influence.

Key problems for presenters

Over the years, I've heard many reasons why people don't like presenting. For example:

- I get nervous.
- I don't like to be the centre of attention.

- I'm petrified by the idea of having to sell on stage.

- Presenting makes me feel out of my comfort zone.

Perhaps you relate to some of these thoughts? Having worked with hundreds of business leaders over the years, I've realised that most of them who struggle to present a compelling message face three key problems:

1. **Their message is too complex.** They know so much about their subject and are so close to it that they think that everything is important. They think they need to communicate *everything*. Most business leaders include too much content in their presentations. They overpack their message and find it hard to simplify. They think their message is simple and clear, but the audience thinks it's confusing. Remember: 'If you confuse you lose' – you lose your audience and their attention.

2. **They follow an uncertain process in developing their presentations.** Many people tell me, 'I've been presenting for a long time, but I still don't know if I'm doing it right.' They lack confidence not in themselves, but in the process. There's a structured way of thinking about presenting. Not following a proven process creates discomfort in front of an audience.

3. **They ignore the negative impact of bad presentations.** The goal of a presentation is not just to share information, but to grab opportunities through effective communication. If you don't plan out how your presentation can generate opportunities, there will be a cost. Businesses lose deals, sales and money because of how leaders and their teams present their ideas. You don't have to be running your own business to see the impact of this. If you're a business leader, you're the face of your company. Bad presentations affect both the image of your company and your credibility. The more this happens, the less confident you are as a presenter.

I understand how hard it is for business leaders to focus on their presentation skills. They think there are other priorities. They feel they have no time. They may think it's not the right time because they need to clarify their message first. Some believe they can improve on their own, while others think nobody can help them – not even a presentation coach. I get it. And I'm glad you're here. I'm glad you made the decision to start (or continue) your journey towards becoming the best presenter you can be.

Confident Presenter will show you a path to be able to present a compelling message, every time. When you present a compelling message, your audience takes action and your business grows. Your audience will also understand your ideas, believe in them, agree with them and remember them. As a result, your ability to influence and your credibility, reputation and career progression will soar.

Three skills to master

If you want to become a more confident presenter, you need three skills:

1. **The ability to develop a clear message.** It requires proper preparation to communicate ideas (which might be complex or technical) in a simple and clear way. In this book, I'll show you how to do that so your audience will be engaged, understand your message and act upon your ideas.

2. **The ability to follow a structured process.** When you follow a proven process, you'll feel more confident. This book will give you a method to help you create powerful business presentations. With the right process, you'll feel more ready than ever to connect with your audience. Presenting will become exciting.

3. **The ability to use presentations to grab opportunities.** What do you want your audience to do after your presentations? The goal of a presentation is to take the audience to the next step. You want to change what your audience believes, feels and, most of all, does. Wouldn't

it be great if your audience acted on your ideas every time you gave a presentation? I'll show you how you can do that.

In our Ideas on Stage training courses and when working with clients, we use the Presentation SCORE method to produce powerful presentations which are Simple, Clear, Original, Related and Enjoyable. My colleague and co-founder of Ideas on Stage, Phil Waknell, explains this method in his bestselling book *Business Presentation Revolution: The Bold New Way to Inspire Action, Online or on Stage*.[1]

I find these five words so powerful that I call them the 'Five Key Principles for Powerful Presentations'. This book will show you how to apply these principles to the content of your presentations in particular. Except for a couple of brief mentions at the end of the book, I'm not going to talk about how to design effective slides or how to deliver your message. This book is about one thing and one thing only: your ability to craft a captivating message. That's the most important factor. If you don't have a compelling message, it doesn't matter how beautiful your slides are or how strong your delivery is. Content trumps everything else.

Ideas on Stage Methodology

Throughout *Confident Presenter*, we will cover and reference several methods and techniques created and owned by Ideas on Stage and laid out in Phil

Waknell's book *Business Presentation Revolution: The Bold New Way to Inspire Action, Online or on Stage*.

The author and publishers fully recognise Ideas on Stage's ownership of these methods and techniques, and Ideas on Stage has given written permission for them to be referenced explicitly or implicitly in this book.

These include:

- The Presentation SCORE Method, or pSCORE for short: a five-stage method for producing and delivering powerful presentations which meet five key success factors, namely: Simple, Clear, Original, Related and Enjoyable.

- The ABC technique: standing for Audience, Burning needs and Context, used to set the foundation for a successful presentation.

- Objective Flows and the Audience Transformation Roadmap: establishing transformational objectives in terms of what you want the audience to do, feel and believe after your presentation.

- What, So what, What next: a simple technique to produce an elevator pitch or a conclusion for your presentation.

Applying the method

The intention of this book is not merely to repeat this method, but to offer simple ways to apply it and bring it to life. It features many real-life examples from my own experience. There's no one right way to create better presentations, but this book describes the best way I know. It will show you how you can change your thinking and gain some genuine confidence. I wrote it because I see a world where every entrepreneur and business leader can share their message with confidence so they can grow their business, increase their influence and make a positive impact in the world.

To get the most from it, first visit www.ideasonstage.com/score and take the Confident Presenter Scorecard to assess how you stand on following the key principles you're about to learn. After you answer a series of simple yes/no questions you'll receive an instant score plus suggestions for improvement. It's free, easy and takes less than three minutes to complete.

Let's get started!

PART ONE
THE FOUNDATIONS OF PRESENTATIONS

Before we can get into the specifics of the Five Key Principles for Powerful Presentations, we need to put some foundations in place. These foundations will help you better understand the principles, why they're important, and make it easier for you to apply the framework in your own context.

In Part One of the book, we're going to look at why complex presentations don't work, and what to do instead; why confidence flows from the process you follow, not from innate self-belief; and why bad presentations are costing you money and/or credibility.

After these foundations, I'm going to walk you through each of the Five Principles in detail, with examples from my own clients.

1
Why Complex Presentations Don't Work

Daniel Priestley, co-founder and CEO of Dent Global, launched a new business in 2020: ScoreApp. ScoreApp is a tool that generates data-rich leads for small businesses and entrepreneurs. The software allows you to set up an online scorecard – much like a quiz – that people fill in and get a customised report based on how they answered the scorecard questions. It's a fun and engaging way to turn cold prospects into warm leads.

In a Facebook group that Daniel manages, I saw somebody asking him the question, 'What's the benefit of using ScoreApp if you already have Typeform?' Typeform is another company that specialises in online surveys. Here's what Daniel said:

'Think of Typeform as a Swiss Army Knife that can do lots of things OK or well enough. Think of ScoreApp as a bread knife that does one thing really well. Sure, you can cut bread with your Swiss Army Knife, but you're going to leave some big crumbs on the bench. Those big crumbs are customers.'[2]

After his analogy, he went on to give some details (not too many) about what you can do with ScoreApp that you can't do with Typeform. Daniel could have chosen to only mention lots of technical features to try and convince the person that ScoreApp is better than Typeform, but that's not what he did. He kept things simple. The most successful messages are the simplest. The best writing gets to the point. The greatest speeches are concise and direct. Too many business leaders fall into the trap of giving presentations which are too complex.

Why does this happen? It's all done for the right reasons. We're talking about experienced professionals who are leaders in their field. The problem is that these experts are often too close to their subject and are too keen to demonstrate their knowledge to their audience. Because they know so much about their subjects, they include too many details. They resort to jargon, acronyms and industry-specific terminology. As a result, the audience can't follow, understand or remember. They are left confused and don't take action.

A key issue is that we rely too much on technology when preparing a presentation. Technology provides us with tools and templates. The latest version of PowerPoint even suggests nice-looking alternative designs. There are thousands of potential shapes to choose from and images to include. The temptation is to throw everything at your slides, including the kitchen sink. But beware, if you go too far, you might find your audience throwing those kitchen sinks back at you. Your ability to deliver a great presentation has nothing to do with the software you use or the screen behind you. It has everything to do with the message you want to convey.

The primacy of the message is backed by how the human brain processes information. Our brain has been evolving for millions of years. We've been sharing stories for generations without the need to put some bullet points on a deck. If you want to communicate a simple and clear message that is relevant to your audience, you must ask yourself the basic question: what does my audience need to hear? You must be ruthless in deciding what to include. Unless it helps you convey your central argument, it must go.

What can you do to get to the point? Here are three practical tips:

1. **Summarise your core idea.** Start by summarising your core idea in seventy words (which should take thirty seconds to deliver). If you can't

communicate it in that short time, your message is too complex. You need to make it simpler.

2. **Decide on one key takeaway.** It's the same tactic which media trainers tell their clients for TV interviews. Stick to the point you want to get across, with no more than three supporting arguments. This gives your presentation a good structure.

3. **Use simple words where possible.** Using fancy language doesn't make you sound clever. It distorts what you're trying to communicate. If there's an easy way or a hard way to explain something, always use the easy way. If there isn't, keep editing until there is. When explaining a concept to a general audience of non-specialists, ask yourself, 'How would I explain this to my grandma?' or, 'How would I explain this to a fifteen-year-old?' That's the language you want to use. If someone doesn't understand a word or concept, they'll stop listening. People don't like to feel like idiots.

As we continue our journey together, I'll show you how you can put these tips into practice. For now, think about your goal. What's your objective when presenting? Maybe you want to sell a product, service or idea. Maybe you want to convince someone of something. Maybe you want to persuade or inspire your audience. Whatever it is, you want to take your audience on a journey from A to B. They'll start at point A where they don't know, believe or feel what you want them to, and travel with you to point B, where they do.

If your message is too complex, it would be like me shouting a foreign language at you and hoping you understand.

If you simplify your message then achieving your objective will be much easier.

2
Confidence Flows From The Process

As a teenager, I was playing football (soccer, for the benefit of American readers) at a decent level. One year we even reached the national final in our league. We played at the Stadio Flaminio in Rome, which can hold 30,000 people. I had never played in such a big stadium before. I was super excited about it, but when the referee whistled for the game to start, my legs froze. I couldn't move. I tried to hide on the pitch as I didn't want to get the ball. I didn't want to make any mistakes. Our coach took me out after twenty-eight minutes (rightly so). I wasn't familiar playing a final in front of so many people, so I wasn't confident at it.

The first time you give a presentation in front of a group of strangers, it can be daunting. The second time, it often goes better. The third time, even better. The more you do it, the more confident you get at it. The more prepared and structured your approach, the more confident you'll be. I see so many business leaders not following an organised process when preparing a presentation. Keen to get started, they launch into things and hope for the best. We've all seen the presenter who decides to wing it. People who do that communicate their message badly, can't sense if their message is landing and lose their audience. This creates frustration – both for the speaker and for the audience. In turn, this leads to insecurity and speakers lose faith in their ability to deliver powerful presentations. It's a vicious circle: the more this happens, the more the frustration and insecurity. To avoid getting trapped into that negative cycle, it's important to plan.

Where confidence comes from

If you want to become a more confident presenter, you need to understand where confidence comes from. Confidence is not something you either have or don't have. It's not something you search for. It's something you develop. It comes from the actions you take and the choices you make. Your inherent ability to speak in public is not what gives you confidence. Your belief that you can succeed at public speaking is not what gives you confidence.

However, you can reinforce your beliefs (and your behaviours as a result) by taking consistent action. Confidence is linked to familiarity. If you want to get confident at something, you need to experience it. In 1986, Queen gave their monumental concert at Wembley Stadium in front of 72,000 people. It has gone down in rock music history as one of the greatest performances of all time. Even a band fronted by Freddie Mercury couldn't have done that at the start of their career. Queen had been touring for over fifteen years by that point. At one gig at Bedford College in 1972, they played to six people. The same principle applies to your presentations. You might not end up at Wembley, but you can improve and build confidence with every presentation.

Many business professionals wish they were natural communicators or feel that they should be. The fact is that presenting is not a natural thing to do. Standing up in front of an audience (on stage or online) takes everyone outside their comfort zone, but you can develop your skills and your confidence to make it look natural.

Following a structured process

If you want to feel confident in your content and in your ability to deliver it, you must follow a structured process. Confidence doesn't come from blind self-belief. Lee Warren in *The Busy Person's Guide To Great*

Presenting: Become a compelling, confident presenter. Every time.[3] explains that confidence comes from three things: 1) Knowing your audience, 2) Knowing your message, and 3) Being prepared.

Before you even start planning a presentation, ask yourself who the audience will be. What actions do you want them to take after the presentation? For example, for an introductory workshop with potential clients, you may want them to express their interest in a follow-up conversation with you or your team. Having established who the audience is, you can think about your message and work on what you want to say. Success in public speaking depends on the process you follow, not on how hard you try.

With a presentation looming, the worst thing you can do is feel you don't have time to prepare and follow a process. Rushing into a presentation and cutting corners will end badly and knock your confidence. If you think you lack time to go through a structured process, think twice. Do you really lack time, or is it possible that sometimes there's a lack of priorities?

One of my clients was Patrick Tyrance Jr, a Harvard-trained orthopaedic surgeon and entrepreneur. He's a busy man. We worked together to refine his public speaking skills while creating a presentation about a new business. Much of our work was about correct preparation. After we worked together, Patrick shared a great analogy. He explained that, as a surgeon, he always goes through any procedure in his mind before he even gets to the hospital. By the time he arrives, he's already prepared and can remain calm for the procedure. His work as a surgeon is more important than any speech, but it's fascinating that he drew those parallels and yet had not recognised the importance of preparing for a presentation in the same way.

3
The Impact Of Bad Presentations

Present a compelling message

One of my favourite brands is Allbirds. Allbirds make sustainable shoes and clothing. Their promise is that their products are as eco-friendly as possible, manufactured using only natural materials. The company is also a certified B Corporation, which means it has the highest sustainability rating. They also say their shoes are the world's most comfortable shoes.

Now, I don't know if they are the world's most comfortable shoes. They certainly feel comfortable to me, but it was their brand values *and* the way they are communicated which made me fall in love with them in the first place. Their key messages – that they are sustainable, comfortable and with a simple design – hit a sweet spot for people like me. Not only do they have a great product, but they've been successful at telling me about it. As a result, I have four pairs of Allbirds: a pair each for the winter, summer, somewhere-in-between and a pair for running.

Allbirds was launched in 2016. By 2020, the company was already valued at $1.7 billion. They went from a small startup to a billion-dollar brand in four years.[4] I'm not saying that product, service or idea isn't important. Of course not. Without an idea there would be no business. Allbirds' shoes are great, but there are other alternatives. There may be rival products which are technically better, but the way they communicate their ideas has touched me and I have no reason to look for replacements. Allbirds understand that having a great product is not enough. They invest considerable time, energy and money on making sure their story, values and messages resonate with their audience.

Not everybody does that. This is true both for companies selling products or services and for business leaders communicating ideas. When you don't present a compelling message around your idea, there's a cost. Bad presentations impact our emotional state, reputation, career and our ability to access opportunities, including financial ones.

Your opportunity to make a great first impression

A presentation is your opportunity to make a great first impression. It's a bit like a first date (only the stakes aren't romantic). The problem is, many presenters fall into the trap of making an invisible first impression. It's not that they create a negative impact, but they fail to make a lasting impact. When a crucial opportunity to make a great first impression doesn't hit the mark and is unmemorable, the negative impact is real and can be quantified.

How do you calculate it? You could analyse how many presentations your company gave in a year, how much time you spent on them and how many of them weren't effective. You could take the average salary of someone in your organisation who had worked on the presentations and work out the hours 'wasted'. But that would be a complicated approach and you also wouldn't come up with an accurate figure.

There's a much simpler way. All you need to do is ask yourself two simple questions: 1) What's the value of a great presentation? The answer is the amount of the deal you're trying to win or the value of the opportunity you're trying to grab. 2) What's the cost of a bad presentation? The answer is the same. The cost of an ineffective presentation is the amount of the deal you didn't win. It's the value of the missed opportunity. On top of that, there are many other factors that often come into play, like loss of staff morale and engagement, reputation damage and career impasse.

CASE STUDY: Surpassing new business targets by more than 40%

Katté & Co is a leading paid search and social agency for ambitious ecommerce brands. Their MD, Tom Katté, was keen for the agency to become more proactive in seeking new business, but they were being held back by their presentations. In their case, a typical client brings in £5,000 per month. They were aiming to convert three new clients a month. Not being able to pitch well and losing that business was losing them a potential revenue of around £180,000 per year.

During a typical pitch, Tom and other senior leaders would focus on the commercials, the strategy and the top-level overview. They would then rely on a team of analysts to go into more depth, but the analysts were a little too technical in their communication and this didn't always work with their potential clients.

Following our training, Tom told me that almost overnight he could see a real difference in the confidence and delivery of content by their analysts. Katté & Co surpassed their new business targets by more than 40%. Engagement and win rates of their pitches have been at a record high ever since.

Stop treating presentations as secondary

One practical thing you can do to avoid the cost of bad presentations is to stop treating presentations as secondary. So many business owners and leaders regard presentations as something 'nice to have' and not a priority. Instead, they devote their time and resources into product development and other business matters.

I get it. Your product or service is the thing you see and work on every day. The way you communicate your offering can be seen as less tangible. Of course, your product or service is important. It forms the core of your business. Without it, your business wouldn't exist, but let me draw a parallel for you. When it comes to publishing content (like this book), experts recommend that you don't just focus on the actual writing. It's also vital to think about how to promote it so as many people as possible will see it. You can write the best book in the world, but without an effective promotion and distribution strategy, no one will read it. And if no one reads it, the whole exercise was pointless.

The same applies to your business. You can have the greatest idea, product or service in the world, but if you can't communicate it, it doesn't matter. You should devote as much time (if not more) on preparing to present your ideas as you spend working on the ideas. Remember, it's the quality of your presentation which will win over an audience, not the ideas themselves.

4
Focus On The Things That Don't Change

Jeff Bezos once said that he's often asked what will change in the next ten years, but almost never what is *not* going to change. He believes that it's the second question which is more important and advises people to 'focus on the things that don't change.'[5] In the case of Amazon, Bezos realised that people will always want low prices, fast delivery and vast selection.

With presentations, we should take heed of Bezos' observation and focus on the things that don't change. The tools and technology we use to communicate our ideas will change. Presentation software will continue to advance. However, the fundamental principles of good presentations will never change. No one is going to come up to you in ten years' time and say, 'Great presentation, I just wish it was more complex/much longer/the structure wasn't that clear/wasn't so rel-evant to me and my needs/more boring.'

Principles first, PowerPoint last

A common mistake is that many business leaders fail to follow set principles for creating their presentations. Some think it's about designing slides on PowerPoint. They believe if they get a decent deck together then they're good to go. If you're one of those people who think that a presentation is about Power-Point (or any other presentation tool), you've missed the point. A presentation is so much more than Power-Point. Focusing on the tool rather than the principles is like worrying about your mic before learning how to sing. What matters is your ability to pitch, present and communicate your ideas so you can achieve your objectives.

Think about it. There are many other areas of life which require us to follow some clear principles – and we would never think to do otherwise. If you want to learn how to play a musical instrument, you would spend time working on fingering or breathing and learning scales. To master a new sport, you would need to know the rules of the game and the basic tech-niques. For racket sports and golf, for example, you would work on your swing. All of that is more impor-tant than having the latest equipment, so why is it that if we want to get better at presenting, we ignore the fundamental principles of communication? A better way to think about this is, 'Principles first, Power-Point last' (or no PowerPoint at all).

The Presentation SCORE method

At Ideas on Stage, we've developed the Presentation SCORE method to create great presentations that meet Five Key Principles: Simple, Clear, Original, Related and Enjoyable.

SIMPLE: Say less and your audience will remember more.

CLEAR: Craft a clear and coherent storyline to keep your audience engaged and inspire them to take action.

ORIGINAL: Present your ideas in a fresh, engaging way to make a lasting impression on your audience.

RELATED: Make your message relevant to the audience. It's not about your idea, it's about how your idea is useful to them.

ENJOYABLE: Keep your audience entertained to increase their attention and retention.

Part One: KEY IDEAS

- Complex presentations don't work. If you want to persuade your audience, keep your message simple.

- Confidence comes from familiarity. It comes from the process you follow, not from innate self-belief. The more you present – and the more you do it by following a proven process – the more confident you'll become.

- The cost of a bad presentation is real and can be quantified. It's the amount of the deal you didn't win. It's the value of the missed opportunity.

- Focus on fundamental principles that don't change.

- The Presentation SCORE method uses Five Key Principles that will help you create a strong presentation.

 One thing

It's time for you to capture what you've learnt so far. What's the one thing you're taking away? It could be anything: an idea, a reflection or an insight. It could be something you've decided to apply in your next presentation. What is it? Write it down in a notebook.

PART TWO
PRESENTING WITH CONFIDENCE

We've seen why complex presentations don't work, how confidence comes from following a process and why bad presentations can hurt your credibility and cost you money. We've also learnt that focusing on principles that don't change is the key to success and been introduced to Five Key Principles for Powerful Presentations used in the Presentation SCORE method. In Part Two, we're going to delve into each of the Five Principles so you can learn how to craft a powerful presentation that will help you inspire your audience, increase your influence and make a bigger impact:

SIMPLE: In Chapters 5 and 6, we're going to look at this fundamental skill – your ability to simplify your message. You'll learn how to overcome one of the main problems in communication: the curse of knowledge. You'll also learn a specific technique to help you simplify the content of your presentations. It doesn't matter how complex or technical your subject is, you must be able to communicate it in a simple way.

CLEAR: Once you've simplified your message, you also need to make it clear. In Chapters 7 to 10, I'm going to cover the juiciest step of all: how to create a clear storyline. You'll also learn why three is the most persuasive number in communication. I'll also give you practical tips to grab the audience's attention right from the start and to motivate them to act on your ideas.

RELATED: In Chapters 11 to 13 we're going to explore the Related principle. You'll learn a specific tool to analyse your audience and a framework for turning boring case studies into captivating success stories that engage the audience. I'm also going to show you a tactic for communicating data so your audience understand the meaning of it.

ORIGINAL and ENJOYABLE: In Chapters 14 to 16 I'm going to show you the last two principles, which go hand in hand. Here, we'll go deep into the power of a story by looking at some practical examples from my own clients. You'll also learn why analogies are so powerful in bringing your ideas to life and I'll show you how to create interactive presentations that engage the audience.

5
The Curse Of Knowledge

In *Made to Stick: Why some ideas take hold and others come unstuck*[6] by Chip Heath and Dan Heath, one of the best books I've ever read, the authors introduce the concept of the curse of knowledge. They cite a Stanford University study known as Tappers and Listeners. In 1990, psychology student Elizabeth Newton asked a series of people to tap out rhythms to famous songs on a table. She invited another set of people to guess the songs. Before the experiment started, the 'tappers' estimated that the 'listeners' would guess the tunes 50% of the time. In fact, they spotted the right songs just 2.5% of the time.

Why was that? The tappers had the songs in their head all the time and couldn't understand how the listeners couldn't identify them. But what the listeners heard might just as well have been Morse code. As Chip and Dan Heath explain, once we know something, we find it hard to imagine what it means not knowing it. That's how it was for the tappers. They define it as knowledge 'cursing' us. When we need to put ourselves in the shoes of someone without our knowledge, unless we make a conscious effort, we don't even realise we have that extra information.

The same thing can happen when presenting an idea. We're in danger of being tappers who assume the audience will be able to recognise the tune. This is especially true when the topic is complex or technical. If you're a business leader or an experienced entrepreneur, I'm sure you've acquired expertise in your field. The problem is that you become so close to your chosen subject area, it's easy to lose sight of other people's levels of knowledge. This can lead to a situation where we think what we're communicating is simple and clear but the audience finds it the opposite.

The curse of knowledge is one of the main problems in communication. Cast your mind back to when you were a student at school or university. There was always a teacher or lecturer with a superb grasp of their subject who wasn't good at explaining it to the class. They were so immersed in their specialist area that they'd lost perspective on how to teach it. Once you've become familiar with this concept, you start to recognise it in different areas of life. Too many writers assume too much of their readers. Sellers don't make enough effort to educate their buyers. Politicians fail to convey their policies and manifestos to voters.

What I see all too often in the field of public speaking is the same mistake: an assumption of too much knowledge among the audience. It's an easy trap to fall into unless you apply some perspective.

Think about what it's like for a top athlete like Usain Bolt. His coach, Glen Mills, is respected in the field of athletics. He has also coached world champion Yohan Blake, and was the head coach for the Jamaican Olympics athletics team. But to look at him, you wouldn't know it. Imagine if the pair of them decided to have a running race over 100 metres. Bolt is lined up in the blocks in one lane and his coach is crouched down in another. The starter fires the pistol and they're off. Who do you think wins the race?

Even though Mills is an experienced athletics coach who has spent most of his life down at the track, I'm pretty sure you would agree that Bolt wins the race. Every day of the week. Yet, Bolt wants Mills as a coach. Why? Because Bolt (like any other top performer) is wise enough to understand that he doesn't know what he doesn't know. He can't see outside his own perspective. Mills may not be the best performer. He gave up sprinting at an early age and switched to coaching. Yet, he has the ability to bring out the best in Bolt. Even a top performer like Bolt needs a reality check and some outside perspective to achieve his peak performance.

The same is true for all of us, no matter what standard we are. It's impossible for us to see what we can't see. It's a universal truth. When it comes to delivering presentations, it's always a good idea to look at things from a different perspective. It helps you see things as others do and this makes you a better presenter. Gaining a different perspective is how you break the curse of knowledge.

CASE STUDY: Avoiding the curse of knowledge

Diana Hudson is Director of Creative Exchange UK, a social enterprise in the creative and cultural industries. She came to me because she had lost confidence in her own ability to deliver talks and training sessions as coherently as she would have liked. Like many people, she found the switch to video calls during the Covid pandemic difficult after years of meeting in person. Diana felt she needed some structure and coherence with her presenting.

We worked on some tactics and methods which she could apply to her work. She found that understanding the needs of the audience was a breakthrough in her ability to break the curse of knowledge. For example, in a presentation about sustainability, she wanted to mention the phrase 'take-make-waste' – a model typical of the linear economy (as opposed to the approach followed in the circular economy). Although the phrase 'take-make-waste' gives the audience some clues about what we mean, to someone who knows little or nothing about this subject, it may not be clear enough unless we explain it.

That's what Diana did. After mentioning the phrase 'take-make-waste', Diana explained that in a linear economy, we take resources from the ground to make products which we use and then throw away. She also gave an example: we take cotton from another country, we use the cotton to make a T-shirt which we wear ten times, and when we're no longer happy with it, we throw it away.

If all she did was mention the phrase 'take-make-waste' without any explanation, assuming the audience would understand it just because she did, she would have complicated her message.

Diana told me she noticed she had become more effective at presenting when she was later asked to speak at a funeral. Several people came up to her afterwards and said how meaningful her talk had been.

Diana says, 'I feel much more in control now that I know how to simplify my message. If I hadn't learnt this principle, I wouldn't have got anywhere close to where I am today.'

Focus on concrete rather than abstract concepts

Next time you have a presentation to deliver, take time to think about how you'll communicate your key messages. Are you assuming your audience has more knowledge than they do? What's the correct level to pitch the talk so everyone can buy into what you're saying? Stop to consider whether your audience will know what you're talking about. There's nothing wrong with breaking things down to their simplest form. That's good communication.

A good way to avoid the curse of knowledge is to focus on concrete rather than abstract concepts. Introduce real examples which will bring your ideas to life. Tell stories to illustrate your key points. People remember anecdotes and examples far more easily than abstract concepts. In Chapter 14, we're going to look at how to use storytelling to make your presentations more engaging, but for now, let's talk about the power of simplicity.

6
The Power Of Simplicity

In 1996, Guinness released their surreal 'Fish on a Bicycle' advert.[7] It finished with the slogan, 'A woman needs a man like a fish needs a bicycle' over a shot of a fish riding a bike. That image has stuck with me. The point being made is that fish don't need bicycles. (And maybe women don't need men.) It's the same with your presentations. Your audience doesn't need everything you think they might.

Keeping things simple is one of the most important principles of effective communication. If you say too many things, your audience will remember very few of them. Keep your presentations short, simple and to the point. While it might seem counterintuitive, taking away details from your presentation will make it stronger and more impactful. Eliminate the unnecessary so the necessary can flourish. This will make it more likely that your audience will understand you, remember your ideas and act on them.

The 'What, So what, What next' model

How do you put all this into practice? At Ideas on Stage, we use the 'What, So what, What next' model to simplify a message. Think about your next presentation. What's your big idea? If you were to summarise the core idea behind your next presentation in one message, what would you say? A useful exercise is to try and distil what you want to say down to seventy words or, to put it another way, how would you sum it up in thirty seconds? If you can't edit your message down to these core seventy words, your message isn't simple enough.

EXERCISE

Write a seventy-word summary of the core idea behind your next presentation using the following format:

- What? What do you want to tell your audience?
- So what? Why should they care?
- What next? What do you want them to believe, feel or do afterwards?

Here are a couple of examples from our clients who have applied this simplification strategy to their presentations:

Richard Mawer, Director of Ignite Growth: With Richard, we prepared a presentation for prospective clients (business owners) titled, 'How to Grow Your Business to Seven Figures and Beyond'.

- **What?** Every entrepreneur can build a successful business.

- **So what?** Most of them have no money, no time and are left feeling stressed, but it doesn't have to be that way.

- **What next?** No matter where you are in your business journey, there's a proven formula that will help you overcome the challenges you face and grow the business you deserve. A business that will give you more fun, freedom and fulfilment.

Paul Spiers, founder of The New P&L Brand Purpose Institute: With Paul, we worked together to prepare a conference keynote to an audience of business leaders titled, 'Why We Need Audacious and Resilient Leadership More Than Ever'.

- **What?** Today's challenges require a seismic shift in the way we think and act as leaders.

- **So what?** Today, people trust brands more than governments to solve many of the challenges we face in society. You have a unique opportunity to take the lead in addressing these challenges.

- **What next?** Everyone in this room can and should do that. It's our collective responsibility to stand up and become the leaders we know we can be.

The 'What, So what, What next' model helps you get to the core of the big idea you want to get across. It also forces you to make it about your audience. When you answer the 'So what' question, you'll make it clear to the audience why your message is important and relevant to them. That's the key to effective communication.

Be kind to your audience

Great communicators use simple words, simple sentences and simple language. In *Book Builder: The definitive guide to writing the book to transform your business*,[8] Lucy McCarraher and Joe Gregory say,

'If there's a hard way or an easy way to say something, use the easy way. If there's a long way or a short way to describe something, take the short route… Do your readers a favour by not assuming they have your level of knowledge – they are reading your book precisely because they don't.'

The same should apply to your presentations. In most cases, your audience is attending your presentation because they don't know as much about the subject as you. Make it simple for them. Be kind to your audience.

Ironically, it's often harder to make things simple rather than complex. That's because it takes work to strip everything down to the basics. Most business professionals use complex language because they think it makes them sound smarter. They fall into the trap of using jargon and acronyms. They use long, confusing sentences.

The best presenters replace complex language with simple words. This doesn't mean your ideas have to be *simplistic*. No one is suggesting you dumb down your ideas or your content. Just make the *language* simple. Carmine Gallo, one of the world's top experts in communication, did an interesting exercise. He took Steve Jobs' presentation when he launched the first iPhone in 2007 and passed the words through the Hemingway App (which analyses language). The first 1,000 words came back as language appropriate for third-grade students (ages eight and nine).[9] That iPhone launch was considered a historic moment for Apple. The technology he was launching was revolutionary, but the language was simple.

CASE STUDY: Simple message, big results

NO PLANET B is an upcycling beauty brand that makes natural, vegan and microplastic-free cosmetics, with no animal testing. Co-founders Jessie and Sebastian Wölke knew they were confident speakers, but their presentations were too long and lacked focus. By their own admission, they used to spend hours tweaking slides on PowerPoint.

After learning the tools and techniques to simplify their message, they revised their approach. After introducing the new tactics, they said that things flowed better from the outset, it was easier to remember what they wanted to say and their ideas carried more weight.

Jessie and Sebastian later told me they had used the tools for two big presentations soon after we'd met. They were able to simplify their messaging, which helped them win new business. With a much clearer and focused concept, they also managed to launch their product in all the stores of an international retailer. This was an amazing milestone, which they attribute to their ability to simplify their message to present their ideas more effectively.

Chapters 5 and 6: KEY IDEAS

- Many presenters fall victim to the curse of knowledge, believing their audience knows more than they do. This hinders clear communication.

- To counter this, you must gain some external perspective to ground yourself.

- When preparing a presentation, take time to think about how to communicate your message to an audience simply and pitch it at the right level for them.

- Summarise the core idea behind your next presentation in no more than seventy words by following the What, So what, What next structure.

- The simpler you can make your presentation, the stronger and more impactful it will be.

 One thing

It's time for you to capture what you've learnt again. What's the one thing that has stuck with you the most in this section? Write it down in a notebook.

7
Three Is A Magic Number

Matthew McConaughey is an extraordinary actor. He's also the author of an incredible book, *Greenlights*.[10] When he won the Best Actor Award for his performance in *Dallas Buyers Club* at the 86th Oscars in 2014, he started his acceptance speech with the following words:

> 'There's three things, to my account, that
> I need each day: one of them is something
> to look up to, another is something to look
> forward to and another is someone to chase.'[11]

There are three things Matthew McConaughey needs each day. Not twelve. Not twenty. Three. And that's how he structured his speech: in three parts.

The Rule of Three

Has it ever become obvious to you during a presentation that your structure isn't clear enough and you're losing the audience? If so, you're not alone. Most presenters struggle with this. The good news is, there's one simple yet powerful communication technique that will help you: the Rule of Three.

Three is the most powerful number in communication. An audience is far more likely to remember information if it's presented in groups of three. If you give your audience one piece of information, they'll feel it's not enough. If you offer more than three, they may find that overwhelming. The advert which launched the original BBC Three channel featured a song by Bob Dorough titled 'Three is a Magic Number'.[12] There's something satisfying about things that come in threes, which makes them highly effective.

Threes are embedded in our culture as easy ways to remember things. Once you realise it, you'll notice it everywhere. Good stories have a beginning, middle and end. Most plays have three acts. Films and books often come in trilogies. Some of the best marketing slogans use just three words, for example: 'Just Do It' (Nike),[13] 'I'm lovin' it' (McDonalds)[14] and 'Every little helps' (Tesco).[15]

The UK government used the power of three for their Covid slogans: 'Stay Home, Protect the NHS, Save Lives'[16] and, 'Hands, Face, Space'.[17] Some of the most powerful political statements also use three: Liberté, Égalité, Fraternité (the national motto of France),[18] 'Life, liberty, and the pursuit of happiness' (from the United States' Declaration of Independence)[19] and, 'Our top priority was, is and always will be education, education, education' (Tony Blair).[20]

Many businesses use a three-tier pricing structure. You often come across bronze, silver and gold price points or service levels. It's no coincidence that we use the same system for first, second and third in sporting events. No one cares who came fourth. The Rule of Three is often used to great effect in comedy. Comedies often have three characters (like the old Englishman, Scotsman and Irishman routines). Even fairy tales often use three for maximum impact, for example: 'The Three Musketeers', 'The Three Little Pigs' and 'Goldilocks and the Three Bears'. Using three words or three phrases for maximum impact appears in many other areas of life. Here are some other examples: 'Ready, steady, go', 'See it. Say it. Sorted' (British Transport Police),[21] and 'sex, drugs and rock n' roll'.

Applying the Rule of Three to presentations

Next time you prepare a presentation, try applying the Rule of Three. Think about the big idea or take-away you want to get across. What are the three points you can use in support of that idea? Break down your structure into three parts. I've never seen a good presentation that can't be divided into three parts. If you aren't paying attention to the way that you structure your presentations, then you're making it hard for your audience to follow you, remember what you say and take action.

To help you understand how you can apply the magic number three to your presentations, here are some examples I've come across in a business context. Feel free to adapt these for your own use:

- Three priorities to achieve our sales target for the next quarter.

- Three reasons to buy our product or service.

- Problem, Solution, Call to action.

- Three benefits to our solution.

- Three reasons why the board should approve the budget for your project.

- Three reasons to hire you.

- Context, Actions, Results.

- Three reasons to invest in our startup.

People often push back about the Rule of Three and tell me they have more than three points to share during a presentation. If you're thinking the same, ask yourself: do you really need to include everything? Are those nine points of equal importance? Of course not. Often, it's better to explain three things that someone will grasp rather than overwhelming them with too much information. Remember, if everything is important, nothing is important. If there really are nine important points, can they be grouped into three sections? Perhaps there are patterns and points of connection? Try combining certain elements so you can still stick to the Rule of Three.

Alan Furley is the co-founder and CEO of ISL Talent, an award-winning UK Recruitment Consultancy. They work as a talent partner to startups and scaleups to help them build strong teams. I worked with Alan to help him create a presentation for prospects on 'How to Get Your First Ten Hires Right'. Alan broke the one-hour presentation down into three key messages, which had some supporting points (also broken down into threes).

The beauty of this technique is that it works all the time. Regardless of how long your presentation is – five minutes, thirty minutes or an hour – you can always structure your content into three parts. I use the Rule of Three myself when I'm running group workshops for our clients. The course includes several sessions and I like to structure the whole workshop into three parts:

- How to craft a captivating message.

- How to reinforce your message with powerful visuals.

- How to deliver your message with confidence.

In 2007, an academic paper titled 'The rule of three: How the third event signals the emergence of a streak'[22] examined people's perception of 'streaks' in stock market movement and sports victories. When something repeats three times, we're most likely to see that as a 'streak'. If it happens more often, we don't place any further importance on it.

The study asked students how much (theoretical) inheritance money they would invest in a stock. The students were prepared to put the most money into shares when they had risen in value over the three previous days. If the stock continued to rise, it didn't make them any more likely to invest. Similarly, book-ies and gamblers place greater weight on teams that have won three games in a row. (If you're into betting, it might make sense to bet against teams that have won three games in a row and back teams that have lost three games in a row to beat the market.)

Three is everywhere.

8
Creating A Clear Storyline

As a teenager who loved football, I was lucky that our coach from my local football team took us to see a live Juventus training session. Juventus being my favourite team, I still remember how excited I was when we took the bus to Turin.

When we got there, we also had the opportunity to attend a training session of the Juventus Academy so we could see how their kids played football. I saw something I didn't expect. In that training session, the Juventus kids never touched a ball, not even once. All they did was running and coordination exercises, which I found a bit boring. I asked our guide what was going on. He explained that they follow that approach for a reason. If you don't know how to run, you can't become a great football player. If you don't have good coordination in your movements, you can't become a great football player. I was stunned, as nobody had ever taught me how to run. It was always taken for granted. During training sessions at my local football team, they just gave us a ball and off we went.

That experience taught me the importance of structure. There are fundamental steps to follow to get to a certain result. First you learn how to run and then you learn how to be coordinated. Only once you've mastered these foundations can you think about learning how to play football.

Following a structure

The same is true for presentations. There's a structure to follow if you want to keep your audience engaged. You must develop a clear storyline that your audience can follow, but most business leaders don't pay enough attention to the way they structure their presentations.

I've come across many presenters who improvise their presentation around some slides. Their 'storyline' is a sequence of predictable slides we've all seen a million times. You know the type of deck I mean. In these formulaic presentations, there's a title slide followed by an agenda slide. (By the way, you'll never capture attention with an agenda slide unless it's surprising in some way. There are far better ways to open a presentation and tell the audience what you're going to cover.)

Then, there's a series of other slides until you reach a conclusion.

Although a lot of work may have gone into it, this kind of presentation is not a storyline. It's just a sequence of slides. There is a *line* of sorts, but there's no *story*. When a presentation doesn't follow any structure, the audience won't be engaged. When the participants leave the meeting, they don't understand what you've said, so they won't remember it and they won't take action. The key messages aren't clear.

The way to avoid these problems is to develop a clear storyline which will take your audience on a journey. If your presentation follows a clear structure, your audience will be able to follow what you're saying and they'll understand and remember your key messages. It's more likely they'll take action from what you've said. Another benefit of having a clear structure is that, as the presenter, you will also find it much easier to remember your key messages. Even if you lose your way in the middle of a presentation and go blank, it's going to be easier to remember what the next section is and get back on track.

The aim of a presentation is to take your audience on a journey from A to B. You want to transport them from not knowing something to understanding it; from not believing to believing; from not feeling to feeling. The journey might persuade them to do what you want them to do. According to Matt Abrahams, a lecturer in organisational behaviour at Stanford University Graduate

School of Business, 'people retain structured information up to 40% more reliably and accurately than information that is presented in a more freeform manner.'[23]

What's the best storyline?

Depending on the needs of your audience and what you're trying to achieve, there are different storylines that work better than others, but there's one structure that works all the time. The diagram below illustrates a structure you can apply to any presentation regardless of the context, the audience or their needs.

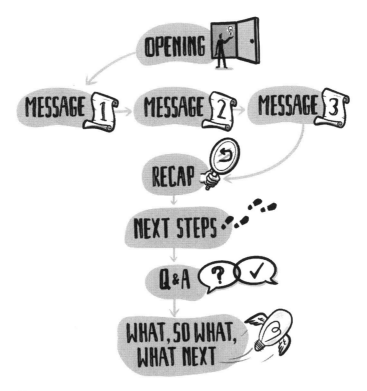

Opening

This is the introduction to your presentation. I use the word 'the' on purpose. This is *the* introduction, not *your* introduction. Most presenters make the mistake of introducing themselves at the start of a presentation. When you start by introducing yourself, you'll never capture the audience's attention. Sorry to break it to you, but no one cares that much about you. Above all, your audience care about themselves and how you can address their needs.

A better way to start a presentation is by making it about the audience. Why should they care? What's in it for them? Why should they listen to you? There are many ways to grab the audience's attention at the beginning of a presentation. I'm going to give you lots of practical techniques in the next chapter. For now, let's continue unpacking the storyline.

Once you've captured your audience's attention and put them first, you can introduce yourself. Here's a format I recommend:

- **Name:** Your name and your job title or what company you're from.

- **Role:** Explanation about what your job entails.

- **Credibility:** What makes you or your company special.

- **Vision:** What motivates you? Why do you wake up in the morning and do the work you do?

I use this personal introduction all the time:

- **Name:** My name is Andrea. I'm the Head of Ideas on Stage UK.

- **Role:** I'm a presentation coach. We specialise in working with business owners, leaders and their teams who want to become more confident presenters.

- **Credibility:** In the last thirteen years, we've worked with thousands of clients around the world, including companies like Microsoft, Lacoste, The World Bank and over 500 TEDx speakers.

- **Vision:** Our mission is to stop great ideas from failing just because of the way they're presented. Our vision is to help hundreds of thousands of business leaders share their message so they can grow their business, increase their influence and make a positive impact in the world.

Main body: Three key messages

The main body of your presentation should be your three key messages and the relevant supporting points. Using the Rule of Three to get your points across is powerful, as seen in the previous chapter.

This is where, in addition to sharing information, facts and figures, you should include stories, examples and analogies. Make sure your presentations include the right mix of logic (facts and figures) and emotion (stories, examples and analogies). These anecdotes are what will make your presentations more original and enjoyable. I know it can be scary to do – especially in a corporate setting – but it pays off. We'll dive deeper on how to use storytelling in business presentations in Chapter 14.

Recap

Now it's time to summarise and reinforce your main message. You've delivered your three key messages in the main body of the presentation. Now summarise the key takeaway.

Don't worry about the fact you're echoing what you've already told them. Repetition is good in communication. If you have an important message to get across and you tell your audience once, they'll forget it. If you tell them two or three times, they'll take it away. What's important is to mix up the delivery and use different words and phrases. It would be boring if your recap was an identical repeat of the same sentences. If you deliver the same message in different ways, that's good repetition. Good phrases you can use to introduce your recap include:

- The message from my presentation is simple…
- My point is this:

- The main point of my presentation is…

The aim of the recap is to focus on the one thing you want your audience to take away from your presentation. Ask yourself what that is. The answer is your recap.

Two important notes:

- Keep your recap as brief as possible. When you summarise your presentation, if it takes more than one breath then cut it back.

- Don't use the word 'summary'. It's a total killer to say something like 'to summarise…'. As soon as an audience hears the word 'summary' they think your presentation is over and stop paying attention. Your presentation doesn't end with the recap.

I mentioned our work with Alan Furley, co-founder and CEO of ISL Talent, in the previous chapter. This is the recap Alan used:

> 'The message from my presentation is simple: every hire is always going to be a risk; you can't get away from that. But by putting some thought, some process and some perspective in place, you can significantly de-risk your hiring so that you'll be confident in viewing your people as an asset, not a liability.'

Next steps

After your recap, it's time to deliver a call to action. What do you want your audience to do after your presentation? What are the next steps? Just like openings, there are many techniques you can use to explain the next steps. It's a crucial and often neglected area. Most presenters don't make it clear to the audience what they want them to do after the presentation or they're not specific enough about the actions.

A presentation is not a mind-reading exercise. You can't expect your audience to know what you want them to do. You need to spell it out and tell them what action to take. Do you want them to express their interest in a discovery call? Tell them. Do you want them to start collaborating with you? Tell them. Do you want them to agree to have a more in-depth conversation with your technical team? Tell them. We'll look at how to do this in more detail later.

Q&A

Another common mistake most presenters make is they include the Q&A at the end of their presentations. They bring their presentations to a faltering finish and say something like:

> 'Um... OK... That's it for today. Do you have any questions?'

Do yourself a favour and don't do that! You should never end a presentation with a Q&A. The Q&A is important because it allows you to interact with your audience and address their concerns, but it's not a good way to finish a presentation. A presentation should end on your terms with your own conclusion. The last point you make should be to state your key message again and why they should care about it. A much better approach is to include the Q&A before your conclusion. Here's how you could approach this:

> 'There's one more thing I'd like to share with you, but I can do that later. For now, I'd be very happy to take any questions. What questions do you have?'

This way, you've signalled to the audience that there will be one more thing to expect, which is your conclusion. If they're interested, they shouldn't leave. Notice the subtle difference between, *'What questions do you have?'* instead of, *'Do you have any questions?'* It's one of those small changes that make a big difference. The first implies that the audience will have some questions and you welcome them. A question is a moment of interaction, and the more you interact with the audience the better. The second implies that they may or may not have questions. It's closing the audience down rather than being open and welcoming.

What if there are no questions?

Have you ever asked an audience if they have any questions and the response is an awkward silence? We've all been there.

It doesn't necessarily mean the audience isn't interested or doesn't have any questions. Sometimes it's just because we haven't given them enough time to think of any yet. A confident presenter always prepares what I call an OSQ.

OSQ stands for 'Oh Shit Question'. It's a question you prepare in advance just in case there are no questions from the audience and you're thinking, 'Oh shit, there are no questions. What can I say now?' If this happens, say something like,

'As you think about your first question, one question I get asked all the time is…'

Then ask yourself the OSQ and you give yourself an answer. You should keep it brief, no more than sixty to ninety seconds. There are three benefits to preparing an OSQ:

- After you've given your answer, it's much more likely that there will be some questions from the audience. You've broken the ice and given them a chance to think.

- You can use this as an opportunity to address an extra point that you couldn't cover in the main body of your presentation.

- Even if there are no questions from the audience after your OSQ, at least you handled this moment with confidence and professionalism. It doesn't feel awkward to you or to the audience. There was at least one question – even if it was from you.

What, So what, What next

Now you've done the Q&A session, it's time for your conclusion – the last words you'll leave your audience with.

This is your opportunity to leave them with the one point you want them to take away from your presentation. The question is: what is it? This is similar to the question I asked you for the recap section. Remember: repetition is good in communication.

A great way to end a presentation is to follow the What, So what, What next format we've covered in Chapter 6. As a reminder:

- **What:** What's the one thing the audience needs to remember?

- **So what:** Why should they care? Why is it important to them?

- **What next:** Now that they care, what do you want them to believe, feel or do?

Here are some suggested phrases you can use to approach your conclusion:

- If there's one thing I'd like you to remember from this presentation, it's this…

- If there's something to take away from this presentation, it's this…

- What I want you to remember is that…

- If you only remember one thing from what we've covered today, here's what I'd like it to be…

Whatever you say next, they will pay attention. I shared Alan Furley's recap earlier. Let's look at how he ended his presentation titled, 'How to Get Your First Ten Hires Right'. Alan said:

'If you only remember one thing from what we've covered today, here's what I'd like it to be…'

(What) 'There's a saying, "Hire slow, fire fast". Please don't. Definitely take time to think about what you're looking for. But once you know that, move quickly, or the best candidates will take offers from somewhere that does.'

'And when it comes to letting someone go, don't rush it. You've made an investment in them; they're part of the team. Sit down with them and work out what's wrong. Connect as a person.'

(So what) 'The reason why this is important is that people are your greatest asset. They're not something you can order off Amazon. Get your hiring right and you'll see a return on that asset rather than viewing it as a cost on the balance sheet.'

(What next) 'To give you something practical you can do with your co-founders tomorrow, create an Org Chart for eighteen months' time [Alan had talked about the value of an org chart in the main body]. Use that to drive your hiring efforts. And of course, if you feel you need any support with anything hiring or talent related, just let me know and I'd be happy to help. Thank you!'

CASE STUDY: Being booked for speaking engagements

I worked with Toby Trimble, MD and founder of Trimble Productions who develops world-class educational programmes for thought leaders in the veterinary industry.

Before working with us, Toby had relied on improvisation too much. He thought that it was a way to come across well, but he'd been listening to recordings of himself giving presentations and felt that he sounded unprepared.

Once we helped him put a clear structure in place, he discovered that it helped him grab the audience's attention and keep them engaged. For example, when Toby would tell a story in the past, he would find it hard to connect it to the real point he wanted to make and build a narrative around it. He also wasn't aware that he could use much fewer details and words to convey the same concept. When he started following a clear structure, he boosted his ability to keep the audience with him.

Toby is also an Assistant Professor of Veterinary Anaesthesia at the University of Nottingham. On many of his lectures, he often tells his own story. Rather than spending five minutes doing that, he's now got it down to less than a minute. Because he's following a clear structure, his communication is much more impactful. He's a better storyteller who helps the audience understand what he's trying to explain.

He's now giving presentations a couple of times a week and being booked for speaking engagements. People have seen him speak and been impressed by the quality of his presentations. Now that he knows how to create a clear storyline, he feels much more confident and empowered to be a proficient speaker who people are excited to listen to.

The power of a good introduction and conclusion

In this chapter, we've looked at an entire storyline from beginning to end. However, keep in mind that the beginning and end of any presentation – in fact, any piece of work – are the most important parts. Research shows that there are two powerful forces at work when it comes to retaining information: primacy effect and recency effect. The information presented at the beginning (primacy) and at the end (recency), regardless of the format, tends to be remembered more than the information presented in the middle.

In *How the Brain Learns*[24] by Dr David A Sousa, an expert in understanding how the brain receives information, he looks at how we retain information from 'learning episodes'. A learning episode is any situation when we take new information on board. It could be a lecture or a presentation. He says we remember best what we learnt first, second best what we learnt last, and least what came in the middle. This even applies to information such as phone numbers – we remember the first digits and the last digits most easily.

Never underestimate the power of a great introduction nor a great conclusion. In the next two chapters I'm going to give you practical tips on how to start a presentation and how to give a clear call to action to motivate the audience to act on your ideas.

9
The Opening

In a Formula 1 race, it's a huge advantage to start in pole position at the front of the grid. The driver who starts in first place is more likely to win because there's no one to overtake. You can apply that analogy to a presentation. If you can get off to a flying start, the rest of the presentation is more likely to go well.

As the philosopher Plato said, 'The beginning is the most important part of the work.'[25] Your opening needs to grab the audience's attention and hold it. Think of two of the most memorable openings to novels which have gone down in history. They are great examples of how to lure people in:

> 'It was the best of times, it was the worst of times…'
>
> *A Tale of Two Cities*, Charles Dickens

'It was a bright cold day in April, and the clocks were striking thirteen.'
1984, George Orwell

While we're not trying to create great works of literature, the principle is the same. Use the first few sentences to create impact. Sadly, most business leaders don't think enough about the way they open their presentations. Instead, they focus on the main body of their presentation and leave the opening to chance. If you don't seize the opportunity to deliver a great opening, you'll lose the audience and it will be hard to win them back.

You only have a limited amount of time to get the audience's attention. In a study which looked at attention span during lectures, students at The Catholic University in Washington DC were asked to use clickers to indicate when their attention was beginning to slip. The study showed that their interest waned after one minute or less.[26] I've read other research which says you have as little as two seconds, seven seconds, thirty seconds, sixty seconds or ninety seconds. The exact amount of time doesn't matter. The point is that you don't have much time. Hook your audience as soon as possible.

The purpose of your opening is to make the audience want to listen. It's your chance to steal an advantage which will remain with you. If you do manage to pique the audience's interest at the start, they'll want to listen to the rest of your presentation. They'll understand why they should care about your message.

Introduction tactics

Here are some suggestions of tactics you can use for your introductions. You could use any of them on their own or combined. The following options also include examples, either my own or from our clients. I've anonymised the client examples for confidentiality reasons.

1. What next

This is the simplest introduction which always works well. It's simple, but a lot better than trying to wing it. You tell the audience what to expect from the presentation: what's coming next, what you're going to cover and what they'll get out of it. An opening for one of my presentations could be something like:

> 'In this presentation, I'm going to cover three main points:
>
> First, we'll talk about how to create a message that captures your audience's attention.
>
> Next, we'll explore how to use visuals to reinforce your message and make it even more powerful.
>
> And then, we'll also work on honing your delivery skills.

'By the end of this presentation, you'll
have a great understanding of how you
can become a more credible, confident and
convincing presenter.'

You can tweak and adapt the underlying format I've
used and apply it to your own presentation. Here's
the format in its stripped back form.

'In this presentation, I'm going to cover three
main points:

Message 1

Message 2

Message 3

'By the end of this presentation, you will…
(this is where you consider what you want the
audience to take away from it. What's your
takeaway promise?)'

2. Context, Problem, Solution

In this type of introduction, you provide a context,
which is the current state of things as it relates to your
message. Then, you introduce a problem before offering a solution to that problem. Here's an example of
this put into practice:

Context: In this presentation, I'm going to talk about
workplace safety.

Problem: We all know that work-related accidents can have a huge impact, not just on employees but also on businesses and the environment. Did you know that in the UK alone, we lost 38 million workdays in 2019 due to work-related accidents?

Solution: The good news is that we can change this. At ABC, we develop user-friendly software that makes it easier to track, identify and eliminate risks in the workplace. We're here to help you reduce your safety risks and I'm excited to show you how our solution works.

3. You want to be… For that, you need… The problem is…

Think about what your audience wants to achieve and start by stating that. Then tell them what they need to do if they want to be successful. Add the tension of a potential problem to get them even more interested. Here's an example:

> 'Thanks for having me here today to talk about how 3D printing can be of value to your business. You said *you want to* understand how it works, and *for that, you need* to know what it can do as a production process. *The problem is,* many engineers still only see 3D printing as a prototyping technology and haven't considered it as a production option. The truth is, 3D printing has evolved and matured to the

point where it's fast, stable and economical enough to be a reliable production process. In this presentation, I'll show you how you can add 3D printing to your production toolbox, giving you a versatile tool that can help take your business to the next level.'

The words for the opening section can change here – it could be 'you want to be' or, as in this example, 'you want to understand'. It's just a matter of starting with what your audience wants.

4. A surprising fact or a shocking statistic

Here, you hit the audience with a striking fact. For example, the introduction above about work-related accidents could be adapted to this style.

'Did you know that in the UK alone, we lost 38 million workdays in 2019 due to work-related accidents?'

5. A relevant quotation

If an authority or an expert in your field has said something interesting and relevant to the message you want to get across, try starting with that. Our client, Alan Furley, started this way:

'Today I'm going to talk about why, as startup founders, you should hire with purpose. As Marc Benioff, the CEO of Salesforce, once said, "The secret to a successful hire is this: look for the people who want to change the world." Let's explore this idea further and discuss how it can benefit your startup.'

6. A thought-provoking question

A great way to kick off a presentation is with a question. It could be your own or it could be one you've found from an influential person. Here are some examples of questions which would be suitable for an introduction that I've found online and in books. I've updated the language from the original material to make it work better in this context and to show how the questions could work:

- *Sourcing knowledge:* 'Imagine a world where we can provide everyone on the planet with access to the sum of all human knowledge for free. What difference would that make? What impact would this have on society and the world as a whole?'[27]

- *Impact entrepreneurship:* 'Imagine if the entrepreneurs of the future acted with a purpose to benefit all instead of only in their self-interest. What if they were rewarded for this? What impact would this have on the world? Today, I'm going to talk about how capitalism has impacted our world and why it's important to adapt it to reflect the values of future generations.'[28]

- *Email outsourcing:* 'What if you never had to check emails again? What if you could hire someone else to spend countless hours working through your inbox instead? This isn't pure fantasy. For the last year, I've experimented with removing myself from the inbox entirely by training other people to behave like me. Not to imitate me, but to think like me. Let me show you how.'[29]

7. A story, metaphor or analogy

This is my favourite technique. Think about the main message you want to convey and ask yourself, 'Is there a story, a metaphor or an analogy that I can use to illustrate my point?' A story, metaphor or analogy is one of the most powerful ways to open a presentation. For example, in one of my workshops – an introduction to becoming a more confident presenter – I start with the analogy that a presentation is like a first date:

'A presentation is an opportunity to make a great first impression. It's like a first date. The problem I see is that most people and companies make the huge mistake of making an invisible first impression when presenting. It's not good or bad; it's just not memorable. We're here to change that! By the end of this workshop, you'll have a great understanding of how you can be a more visible, impactful and confident presenter.'

Now that we've looked at various options for great openings, here are three final tips to consider:

- Invest time in preparing a great opening. Don't ignore this step. It's often what determines whether the audience will want to keep listening.

- Once you've prepared it, internalise it. Rehearse the introduction multiple times until you know exactly what to say.

- Before you start your presentation, focus only on your opening. Athletes are taught to only think about their first step as they're waiting for a race to start. You can apply the same technique. Don't think about the rest of the presentation. Just keep repeating that opening section to yourself. If you've rehearsed the whole presentation, the rest will take care of itself.

REHEARSE
AND INTERNALISE

INVEST TIME AND
PREPARE

FOCUS
(ONLY ON YOUR OPENING)

10
The Next Step

If there's a common purpose to most presentations, it's to persuade the audience to act on your ideas. You want to take them to the next step. The best way to persuade the audience to do what you want them to do is with a clear call to action. If the call to action isn't clear enough, the audience will fail to act. Your presentation will have been in vain.

This was Leonardo DiCaprio's call to action during his speech at the 2014 United Nations Climate Summit in New York City:[30]

> 'This is the most urgent of times, and the most urgent of messages… The time to answer humankind's greatest challenge… is now. We beg you to face it with courage. And honesty.'

In the previous chapter we looked at how to start a presentation. Now let's have a look at how to give a clear call to action. In this chapter I'm going to suggest seven components which make up a perfect call to action to help you bring about business success. First, let's look at some of the most common mistakes I see business leaders make when it comes to their calls to action.

The most common mistakes

1. They think their objective is to share information. If your objective is to share some information then make a phone call, write an email or draft a report instead. There's no need to give a presentation if your only objective is to share information.

The main purpose of a business presentation is to change your audience and inspire them to act on your ideas. You want the audience to believe that the action you're advocating is worth taking for them – not just because it benefits you.

2. They don't include a call to action. Some presenters are so close to their material. They know what *they* want, so they assume the audience will too. This is the typical mind-reading presentation: the person delivering it expects the audience to be psychic. It doesn't work like that. The audience doesn't have a crystal ball. You need to be clear about what you want them to do and you need to tell them.

3. They include an ambiguous call to action. Another mistake is failing to make the call to action specific enough. People make their requests too ambiguous. For example, imagine you were giving a webinar or an introductory workshop on your area of expertise. The objective is for the audience to sign up for a discovery call to see if you can work together. Most presenters say something like:

'If you think you need a bit of help on (their area of expertise), I'm happy to offer a discovery call.'

The problem is that even if someone was interested in a discovery call, they don't know how to book one in, so they won't. The call to action isn't specific enough. Many presenters miss out on an enormous amount of business opportunities because their calls to action aren't specific enough.

Key components of an effective call to action

Now that we understand the key mistakes to avoid, let's break down the key components of an effective call to action. These characteristics are mainly relevant to sales presentations but you'll be able to learn something here for any presentation. After all, all business presentations are selling something – whether it's a product, a service, a project or an idea.

You don't need to use all these elements. See what works for you, based on your audience, the context and what makes you comfortable.

1. Be specific. Here's how the above example, with the vague offer of a discovery call, could be better phrased:

> 'If you enjoyed this session and you'd like to learn more about what we've covered today, at the moment I have an opportunity for three complimentary consultations to see if there might be a fit between what you're looking for and what we have to offer. Regardless of whether or not there's a good fit, I can promise you that you'll walk away with much greater clarity on how you can…' (complete with whatever your presentation is about, eg, be a confident presenter).

In the case of an online presentation:

> 'If you're interested, just type "yes" in the chat now and I'll get in touch to see if you qualify. If you do, we'll arrange a time for a call.'

People know what they have to do to signal their interest. They need to type 'yes' in the chat section. It's a small change that makes a huge difference.

2. Include a logical next step. It's often inappropriate to move into full-on sales mode during an initial presentation – especially at something like an educational webinar or an introductory workshop on your area of expertise. What's an alternative logical next step?

The best approach is one which makes sense to the audience based on where they are right now. It could be that the audience books or expresses their interest in a consultation or discovery session. You could invite them to complete a quiz to find out the areas in which they perform well and the areas they need to improve. Alternatively, you could offer them access to some free resources to learn more about how you can help them in return for their contact details.

The possibilities are endless. What's important is that you're clear about the logical next step, which may or may not be a sale. In Ramit Sethi's book *I Will Teach You to Be Rich: No guilt, no excuses - just a 6-week programme that works,*[31] he says:

> 'The way you get people to floss is to just ask them to floss one tooth… Their brains say, "I'm the type of person who likes to floss."…After a few weeks they are flossing all of their teeth because their brain sees it wasn't as hard a habit as they thought.'

Your next logical step should follow this principle of leading your audience at an appropriate pace towards your end goal. Start with one tooth and take it from there.

3. Include an immediate next step. Not only does the next step need to be logical, ideally, it should also be immediate. If you ask the audience to type 'yes' in the chat during a webinar or to fill out a form during an in-person workshop expressing interest on the spot, that's immediate. Always try to think how to make the next step as immediate as possible, even when it seems hard to do.

I once saw a speaker at a conference get hundreds of people to sign up for a follow-up conversation in an unambiguous way. He could have just flashed up his email address on screen and invited people to message him. Instead, he asked everyone to unlock their phones, open up their email app, type in his email address and a specific subject line and hit send. It was a bold move, and not for everyone, but it worked for him. Perhaps you won't be so direct, but think about how you can make your call to action more immediate.

4. Sell the opportunity. You have something valuable to offer to those you seek to serve. Don't be shy about it. This is an opportunity for them. Of course, it helps you and your business too, but it also helps your audience. Frame what you want your audience to do as an opportunity for them rather than as something you need from them. Language matters and using a phrase including the word 'opportunity' can be powerful.

'If you enjoyed this session and if you'd like to learn more about how what we've covered today could work for you, at the moment *I have an opportunity* for three complimentary consultations…'

5. Create scarcity and/or urgency. In the example where the presenter is offering complimentary consultations, it's limited to three. This helps to create tension. If everybody can reserve a consultation, there's no tension. If only three people can do it, it helps to drive demand for your offer.

This works in person if you ask participants to fill out a form and others can see them doing it. It also works in a webinar or video presentation where everyone can see the chat responses. If ten people all signal their interest, knowing there are only three spaces, that creates the tension you're looking for.

To create yet more tension, you can also say that the opportunity has a time limit, for example, the free consultation might expire in two or three days. Of course, this must be genuine or you'll undermine your credibility. You don't want to be salesy and pushy. As an example, you could work out how many consultations you need to have (and how often) to hit your sales targets. If you know you need to have three consultations after each presentation and you give one presentation per week, that provides the urgency and scarcity.

6. Give reassurance. It's helpful to soften your call to action by offering reassurance that there's no obligation or pressure. Make it clear that the audience is expressing interest rather than committing to anything more.

> 'Regardless of whether or not there's a good fit, I can promise you that you'll walk away with much greater clarity on how you can…'

What the presenter is saying here is that it may or may not be a good fit. They may or may not end up working together. Either way, it doesn't matter.

7. Make sure it's not confusing. Resist the temptation to include too many elements in your call to action. You only need one next step and I would never include more than two. No one wants to book a follow-up call, download a report, take your quiz, read your article, join your private Facebook group and buy from you today. This is confusing. The result of asking for too much is that the audience will do nothing. Choose one logical next step and stick to it. You could have a secondary call to action, but that's it. No more than that.

CASE STUDY: A 'brilliant technique'

Paul McCluskey is the founder and Managing Director of Gemstone Legal. He told me that his presentations were failing to deliver the impact he needed and he wasn't realising his potential, so his confidence was suffering. When preparing presentations for an audience of Finance Directors and Managing Partners of various law firms, he was relying on too many bullet points and was suffering from 'analysis paralysis'.

He worked hard on the structure of his presentations and learnt how to develop a strong narrative and a powerful message. He also learnt how to include a simple, clear and specific call to action which he says has delivered 'unbelievable' results for him. He described it as a 'brilliant technique' to take his audience to the next step, which helped him create a higher level of engagement. Paul went from feeling uncomfortable making presentations to being proud of what he delivers. His confidence has soared and he has won new business. He has even applied some of the techniques he learnt to his wider business model and he told me he's super excited about it.

How to adapt your call to action for online presentations

Remember those days before Covid? It was less common to give an online presentation, even though the technology existed. If you're presenting in person, you can leave your call to action until the end. However, in an online environment, it's better to repeat your call to action twice: once near the beginning and again at the end.

It's much harder to control the room over a video call. Audience members can log off at the click of a button or turn off their cameras. You don't want their Wi-Fi to stop working or for them to slip away to feed their pets just as you're delivering that crucial call to action!

The first time you mention it (after you've covered some of your key points), it doesn't have to be specific. You must earn the right to give a call to action. Offer the audience some value first. At this point, say something like:

> 'Before we continue, let me take a few seconds to mention something that might be of value to you. If you're interested in these ideas then please stay tuned, because at the end of this session I'll give you the opportunity to express your interest in a free consultation. I'll give you more details later. For now, let's continue.'

Here, you're just teasing the call to action which will be coming at the end. People know what to expect and, if they're interested, they know they shouldn't log off or they'll miss out.

I've given countless webinars over the last few years and discovered that if I repeated the call to action twice, I got a much higher conversion rate. It's the same with websites and landing pages. Marketeers include repetitions of the same call to action on a landing page for the same reason: the conversion rate goes up. Of course, a presentation is not a landing page. You don't want to repeat it ten times, but the same principle applies. You just need to tweak it.

EXERCISE

Now it's time for me to deliver a call to action to you. For your next presentation try the following tips:

- Think about your objective. What do you want your audience to do? Write it down.
- Prepare a clear and specific call to action.
- Make sure it meets most of the characteristics above.

Chapters 7 to 10: KEY IDEAS

- The power of threes:
  - Our brains are wired to find the Rule of Three satisfying. We retain three pieces of information more easily than any other quantity.
  - Using the Rule of Three in your presentations is super-powerful. Any presentation can be structured into three parts.

- The importance of structure:
  - Having a clear storyline will elevate your presentations and ensure that your audience understands and remembers your key messages.
  - The opening of a presentation is your chance to grab the audience's attention. Don't waste time introducing yourself or showing an agenda slide. People aren't interested in you. They care about themselves, their needs and how you can help them.

- Aim not to inform, but to generate action:
  - The purpose behind most business presentations is to encourage an action from the audience. The aim is *not* to share information, so include a compelling call to action.

 **One thing**

It's time for you to capture your lessons again. What's the key insight you're taking away from this section? Write it down in a notebook.

11
Audience First

When Paul McCartney headlined Glastonbury in 2022, he played a long set which included lots of newer material, plus songs from his 'Solo and Wings' album. Many people loved it, but he was criticised for not giving the audience what they wanted – which was the hits. No doubt Sir Paul had his reasons. He doesn't just want to play Beatles songs all evening. But even someone of his experience and talent can get it wrong sometimes.

It's an easy mistake to make. I see lots of business leaders giving presentations which are not relevant to their audience. As a result, the people on the receiving end don't react the way the speaker wants them to. To explain why this happens, let me ask you a question. If you had to give a presentation in a few weeks' time, what would be the first thing you would start working on? Don't tell me what you *should* be doing. Be honest and think about what you would actually do.

The first thing many business leaders do is boot up their laptop, open a presentation tool and start working on a deck. Others might stop to think about their message, their objective or the outline. That would be a better approach, but even that isn't the first thing you should do. The very first step you should take is to think about the audience. As my colleague Phil Waknell points out in his book *Business Presentation Revolution*, when you give a presentation to an audience, it's *their* presentation, not yours. It's always the audience's presentation. This means that you need to start with *them*. You need to put the audience first.

Putting it into practice

At Ideas on Stage, we have an easy way of going about it. We always start with the ABC of preparation. ABC stands for Audience, Burning needs, Context. Before you do anything else, you need to take some time and ask yourself some questions about these three areas. *Business Presentation Revolution* includes a more detailed summary of the questions you might want to consider, but here's a recap of some of the most important questions from Phil Waknell's book:

Audience

- Who are the key people in the audience?
- Which company do they work for?
- What are their job titles?

Burning needs

- What are their main questions and challenges?
- How do their questions and challenges relate to your presentation?
- What do they expect from your presentation?

Context

- How long should the presentation be?
- How many people will you be presenting to?
- In what room will your presentation take place?
- If it's online, what conferencing tool are you going to use?

As an exercise, in preparation for your next presentation, use a table like the one below to write your answers to the questions above.

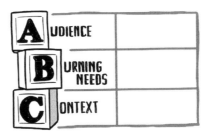

I remember an episode of 'The Simpsons' where Homer buys Marge a bowling ball for her birthday. She isn't happy, because she's never bowled in her life. Marge complains that he only purchased it for himself, and she's right. The bowling ball even has Homer's name engraved into it![32] When you prepare a presentation, don't be like Homer. Don't start by thinking about yourself, what your message is and what you want to get out of it. Start by reflecting on your audience. That's how you develop presentations which are *related* to your audience.

The audience

When I talk about the importance of starting with the audience, I often get asked, 'What if I don't have all the answers?' It's not always possible to know everything about your audience. You might be able to make some assumptions based on your industry experience, but there might be gaps in your knowledge about their burning needs and the context. The more you can get to know your audience in advance, the more solid your assumptions will be.

Not all the questions will be relevant each time you prepare a presentation, but the process of running through them, researching as much as you can and thinking about the audience's needs and the context is always time well spent. The answers to the questions will help you develop a message which is relevant and useful for the listeners. It's impossible to create a presentation which is related to your audience unless you start with the ABC.

When I coach people about the need to analyse the audience, another question I often get is, 'What if I have a mixed audience?' It's a good question because the audience is not always going to be made up of people in the same situation. They might have different levels of knowledge and different expectations and needs. When you have a mixed audience, ask yourself three key questions (in this order):

1. Who is your main audience? There may be people with different roles, from different departments or with different needs. The question you need to ask is, 'Who do I really want to reach?' If there's one person or subgroup of people which represents your target audience then aim your content at them.

2. What are the key messages that will be relevant to the majority of the people in the audience? Another approach is to think about the *majority*. As Emma Ledden points out in *The Presentation Book: How to Create it, Shape it and Deliver it!*[33] when you deal with a mixed audience, you need to accept that you won't be able to please everybody. And you shouldn't try to. When you try to please everybody, you run the risk of pleasing nobody. Think about the key ideas that will resonate with the *majority* of the people in the audience and focus on those.

The first time I ever stayed abroad for any length of time was in Sligo (Ireland) for an international student exchange programme. We were a group of students who had come from all over Europe. If I had tried to speak in different languages in a group situation to try and fit in with who I was speaking to, it would have always alienated someone. We had to find common ground or it would have been chaotic. Of course, English was the language that most of us understood. Focus on what works for the majority of the audience.

3. Can you create a modular presentation? If you've considered everything and concluded that you do need to try and address everybody, you could create a modular presentation where you split your speech into several sections. Each section is designed for a particular subgroup of the audience.

For example, let's say you need to give a sales presentation about a product you want to supply to a prospective client. In the audience you'll have the Product Owner, the Supply Chain Manager and the Head of Purchasing from your client's organisation. To reach these three subgroups, you could have a section about the features and benefits of your product, explaining how it fits into their product strategy. You could have a second section covering logistical questions and a third one could be about the commercial aspects. Tell the audience at the start that you've split your presentation into these three sections so they know what to expect and when they'll be required to pay more attention.

Remember your ABC of preparation. As you prepare your next presentation, before you do anything else, spend some time analysing your audience, their burning needs and the context. Make it about them.

.

12
It's Their Story, Not Yours

Picture this. You're at a party having fun with some friends. You think it would be a good idea to meet some new people. You see a group in the corner of the room and you think, 'Let's give it a try.' You approach them and find your way into the conversation. At first it all seems fine, but after a while, you realise you're stuck. There's one person in the group bragging about his own achievements all the time. He's always done everything anybody mentions and keeps bringing the conversation back to himself. There's no space for you and the others to participate. It's so tedious that you just want to walk away.

In communication, you're that person when you make it about you. The audience wants to get up and leave. This is also true when it comes to sharing examples, stories or case studies in a business presentation. One of the worst things you can do is to make them about yourself instead of the client or the audience. I've seen it so many times. I hear phrases like:

- We've been the industry leader since 2010.

- We have 123 offices in 36 different countries.

- We have 7,500 clients across 80 industries.

- We're a pioneering company in our field.

- We offer the most complete and mature solution in the market.

- We make the world's best cup of tea.

It's all about how wonderful *we* are. The problem with this approach is that it doesn't create a good connection with your audience. In fact, it creates distance.

A more subtle mistake people make when telling stories or sharing case studies is failing to frame them in a narrative that includes the audience. In not doing so, we make ourselves, our brand, our company or our product the hero of the story. But nobody cares about us. Above all, our audience care about themselves and their needs. You should tell stories that make them understand how your brand, company, product or idea can help them get what they want. You should relate your stories to the client or the audience and make it more about them. It needs to be *their* story, not yours.

In the previous chapter, we applied a similar approach to your whole presentation. I discussed how you need to make it *their* presentation, not yours. It's always the audience's presentation. When you tell a story, the same principle applies. It's *their* story, not yours. In *Building a StoryBrand: Clarify Your Message So Customers Will Listen,*[34] Donald Miller says the client must always be the hero of the story. Your role should be that of a guide who gives the hero a plan, product, service or solution that helps them get what they want. The way to achieve this is to transform your case studies into narratives from the perspective of the real hero: your client. The client has a problem. A guide (you, your company, your product) comes along and provides the solution that helps them achieve success. There are two key elements which make this a great approach:

- It's a narrative, which means that it follows a story framework. That makes your communication far more engaging, relatable and memorable.

- It's told from the perspective of the client. It's not about your success; it's about the success of your clients. The client is the hero.

A four-step framework

How can you put these ideas into practice, even if you're not a natural storyteller and don't know how to start? The simplest way I've found to implement this comes from the book *Seven Stories Every Salesperson Must Tell* by Mike Adams.[35] He shares a straightforward, four-step framework:

1. Setting

2. Complication

3. Turning point

4. Resolution

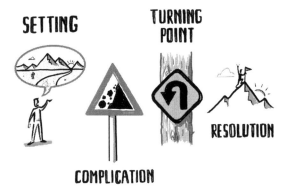

1. **Setting:** All you need to do at the start is mention time and place. For example, 'Three years ago we worked with ABC in London.' When you start a message with time (three years ago) and place (London), the audience knows you're about to tell them a story.

2. **Complication:** This is where you describe what your client's problems were. What challenges and obstacles was your client (the hero) experiencing before they met you?

3. **Turning point:** This is where you come along, not as the hero of the story, but as the guide. Explain how you helped your client solve their problem.

4. **Resolution:** Now put a spotlight on the success of your client. What did *they* achieve because of your help? Remember: it's about them. It's their story and success, not yours.

Let's have a look at a practical example. I worked with a business leader at Circulor, a London-based B Corp which uses technology to help their clients make their supply chains ethical, traceable and sustainable. Here's a success story she included in a presentation we developed together:

1. **[Setting]** 'Let me give you an example of a well-known brand that's already using our technology to improve their supply chain. Three years ago, we started a first pilot with a global company that needed to source batteries for their operations in Rwanda.'

2. **[Complication]** 'The problem is that batteries use rare earth minerals that are only mined in places like Rwanda or Democratic Republic of the Congo, where some suppliers have human rights issues and other ethical problems. The brand cares about their corporate responsibility and the last thing they want is to be associated with a major disruption or scandal.'

3. **[Turning point]** 'They decided to try our solution for mapping their complex supply chain for batteries. The technology gives unprecedented traceability, promotes sustainable practices and better transparency for their customers.'

4. **[Resolution]** 'This pilot strengthened their commitment to an ethical supply chain and paved the way for the entire raw materials industry to produce truly sustainable products. This project was so successful that our client expanded the use of our technology into other areas of their operations and they're contributing to a more sustainable business.'

Making it about 'them' in other contexts

Remembering to move the focus away from yourself can be useful on other occasions as well – even when telling your own story. If you want to introduce yourself during a presentation, sales conversation or meeting, use the same structure. Here's how I would use this format to tell my story (which you may recall from the introduction of this book):

'Hi. My name is Andrea. I'm the Head of Ideas on Stage UK. I'm a presentation coach.'

[Setting] 'The reason why I'm so passionate about public speaking is because, as a little kid growing up in Italy, I was surrounded by small business owners. My parents have always run their own business. They still do. Growing up in that environment, I saw their challenges (raising four kids while trying to run a business isn't easy), but I also saw their spark, entrepreneurial mindset and proactive approach to life. That's why I always wanted to be an entrepreneur.'

[Complication] 'In reality, that remained a dream for a long time. Before doing what I do now, I tried many things and started many projects. All of them failed, but that's what helped me see that great ideas often fail not because of the idea itself, but because of how it's communicated.'

[Turning point] 'That's why I became a presentation coach. That's why my mission is to stop great ideas from failing just because of the way we present them. My mission is to help business owners, leaders and their teams become the best presenters they can be so they can grow their businesses and increase their influence.'

[Resolution] 'I see a world where every business leader can use the power of their message, their story and their voice to make a positive impact in the world.'

According to a Deloitte study, 'Client-centric companies are 60% more profitable compared to companies not focused on the customer.'[36] If you relate your content to your audience, you'll take your communication to a higher level. When you elevate your communication skills, you'll also take your business to a higher level.

EXERCISE

Here's something to get started. Go back over all the examples, stories and case studies you use in your communications (whether that be on your website, in your marketing materials or your presentations) and assess them against the story framework you've learnt here. Ask yourself:

- Is the setting clear?
- Have I explained the complication from the perspective of the client?
- Is it clear that my role is not the hero, but a guide who supports the hero (my client)?
- Is the resolution about the success the *client* has experienced?

If you answer no to any of these questions then turn your stories into powerful narratives that follow this framework. Your communication and your business will soar as a result.

13
Show Me The Data

In 2022, my wife and I had Kian, our first child. During her pregnancy, we attended a training course for new parents organised by the NHS (the UK's National Health Service). At some point, the nurse was trying to explain to us how big (or tiny) a newborn's stomach is. She said that on day one, it's 5-7 ml (the equivalent of the size of a cherry). After one week, it will be 45-60 ml (the equivalent of an apricot). After one month, 80-150 ml (the size of a large egg). I was struck by how brilliant her comparisons were and how they made the information relatable. Millilitres are hard to get your head around, but a cherry, an apricot or an egg? I get it! Also, how incredible that a baby's stomach grows at that rate.

Data and numbers can be important to a business presentation, but they can be bone-dry unless you bring them to life in interesting ways. I often see business leaders struggle to communicate data effectively. When I ask them if they think they're doing it well they say yes, but often that's not the case. Too many presenters assume that their data is meaningful, per se. 'Here's the data: take it, use it, understand it, remember it.' That's how we often communicate data but it doesn't work like that.

As presenters, it's our responsibility to communicate data so that it means something to the audience. The way to do that is to tell the story behind the data. Data alone is not meaningful unless we turn it into insight. If we can turn data into insight, it can become a powerful tool to drive action from the audience.

Making it relatable

Nancy Duarte, CEO of Duarte Inc, explains that there are three ways to put data into perspective. In her book *DataStory: Explain Data and Inspire Action Through Story*,[37] she gives this advice: connect data to relatable size, time and things. You make data *relatable* by putting it into perspective and making it familiar to the audience. Let's put this into practice.

Connecting data to relatable size

In this context, size refers to length, width, height, thickness or distance.

One of our clients wanted to communicate how their software had saved their customers from driving 250,000 miles. Their application allowed workers to do certain tasks remotely instead of having to travel to specific locations.

They decided to try and help the audience visualise how great that distance was. They likened it to driving the length of Great Britain (which is around 600 miles) more than 400 times. It was a compelling way to bring the 250,000 miles to life in a relatable way. Everyone in the UK can understand what it would be like to drive between Land's End and John o' Groats 400 times.

Their first idea was to say that they had saved the equivalent of travelling around the world five times. That would have been OK, but the previous example is more relatable. If you've never circled the Earth, you'll find it hard to understand what that means. Anyone in the UK will have an idea of how far it is from Scotland to Cornwall. It's always about the audience.

Connecting data to relatable time

Time is an excellent way of putting data into perspective, especially when it comes to explaining the value of money.

Another of our clients wanted to communicate that she'd sold 100,000 units of her product in the previous three years. She was keen to demonstrate that there was high demand for her product. She broke the figure down to (more or less) 100 products sold every day. Again, much more relatable.

Connecting data to relatable things

You can also put data into perspective by connecting it to things that are familiar to the audience.

For example, I stumbled upon a video by National Geographic[38] which explained that the blue whale is the largest living animal to have ever existed. The largest blue whales can be more than 100 feet (30 metres) long.

To help people visualise 30 metres, they said that it's the same length as three school buses. Imagine three school buses put together. The blue whale is as large as that! What a perfect way to make that relatable.

Tell the story behind the data

In addition to putting data into perspective, another technique you can use is to bring out the story behind the data.

I worked with Eileen Hutchinson, founder of NitNOT, a company that makes head lice treatments. You might have seen Eileen on the BBC show, *Dragons' Den*, introducing her product. In the presentation we worked on, Eileen argued that most head lice treatments are ineffective and dangerous. According to the Medicines and Healthcare products Regulatory Agency (MHRA), there were ten serious burn injuries caused by head lice eradication products before 2018.[39]

This is already alarming for any parent who's experiencing this issue in their family, but we can bring data to life by telling the story behind it. In this case, Eileen recounted the example of a young student from Bradford who suffered a freak accident when her head lice shampoo caught fire. She suffered third-degree burns on her face and body and lost seven fingers. It required hundreds of surgical procedures for her to recover and rebuild her life.

If you want to convince an audience that some head lice treatments are dangerous, wouldn't you agree that a real story of a real person is more powerful than a naked number?

CASE STUDY: Making data more relatable

Ollie and Jack Farrer, the co-founders of paid media agency Farrer, wanted help to communicate their data in a more engaging way. They wanted to get better at running meetings, making pitches and presenting proposals with lots of data in them.

Ollie and Jack were keen for their team to improve their proposals so they would stand out, win bigger clients and become more confident at communicating their ideas.

The Farrer team came along to one of our workshops and one of the focal points was making data more relatable.

Before attending the session, they used to include big tables of data on their slides – piling everything onto one page – which often confused the audience. Now, they only include the most important metrics. This forces the team to explain the data that makes sense to their clients. As a result, it prompts clients to listen.

They also make sure they put their data into context. For example, let's say they want to convince a potential client to implement a more in-depth conversion funnel. Instead of just saying that this tactic can boost website traffic by 600,000 views per year, they now say that 600,000 views are equivalent to over 1,600 views every single day. Or that this is enough people to fill over six Wembley Stadiums to capacity. Imagine having six Wembley Stadiums full of people and all of them are there because they want to browse your website.

Ollie and Jack told me that the workshop has energised their team. They now look forward to communicating data, making proposals and pitching ideas.

For your next presentation, every time you want to communicate some data, ask yourself:

- How can I put it into perspective?

- How can I extract meaning from my data?

- How can I communicate it so it makes sense to the audience?

- How can I communicate the data so it means something to them?

A good technique is to complete the following sentence: '(Your number) is equivalent to…' and choose a size, time or thing like the previous examples:

- 250,000 miles is equivalent to driving the length of Great Britain more than 400 times.

- We sold 100,000 products in the last three years, which is equivalent to 100 products per day.

- 30 metres is equivalent to three school buses.

If you can draw these relatable comparisons then you can unlock the power of data to tell your audience something they didn't know before, that they didn't see before or that they didn't understand before. This is how data can drive action.

Chapters 11 to 13: KEY IDEAS

- Many business leaders start preparing for a presentation by working on their slides or on their message.

- The best action to take before anything else is to think about your audience. You can do this by following the ABC of preparation: Audience, Burning needs and Context.

- From now on, whenever you want to include a story in a presentation, relate it to your audience. Your client is the hero of the story, not you. Your role is that of the enabler who helps the client achieve success.

- When communicating data, bring it alive by making it relatable. Put data into perspective by connecting it to size, time or things which the audience understands. If you learn how to present data well, then your business presentations will be more effective and you'll reap the rewards.

 One thing

It's time again for you to capture what you've learnt in this section. What's the one thing you're taking away? Remember, it can be anything: an insight, a reflection or a new idea ready to be applied. Write it in a notebook.

14
The Art Of Storytelling

In 2021, Susanna Lawson, founder of OneFile, gave a presentation about women's confidence. She decided to include a personal story about her own experience. Susanna had founded the apprenticeship software company with her husband. They delayed starting a family while they focused on the business. Aged twenty-nine, when the company had grown, they had their first son and Susanna took a year off on maternity leave. By the time she returned to work, the company had doubled in size from nine to nineteen employees. She said:

> 'Before having our baby, I wasn't really
> maternal. I told the team I would be back in a
> couple of months. But once he came, I knew
> I needed to be off for longer and we agreed

I would take a year. In that year, OneFile doubled in size because it coincided with massive improvements in technology.

'First, I came back to work part-time. After a couple of weeks, I overheard a couple of the new team members. One of them asked, "Who is she?" and the other replied, "Oh, she's the boss's wife." I was devastated. I felt like I had been punched in the stomach. I wasn't the boss's wife. I was the boss! But they didn't see me as that. My confidence was in tatters. I've rarely cried at work, but this was one of those times.'

The story was a powerful and personal way to explain her own relationship with confidence and every woman in the audience could relate to it. If you want to connect with an audience, one of the most powerful strategies is to share stories and real-life experiences. Facts and figures are hard to remember but we love hearing anecdotes.

Many presenters make the mistake of only sharing information. They include abstract concepts, facts and figures, so their presentations remain dry, factual and boring. You don't want to be a boring presenter. As Dr John Medina says in his brilliant book *Brain Rules*,[40] 'The brain doesn't pay attention to boring things.'

So far in the book, we've explored making sure you keep your message as *simple* as possible, how to present a *clear* message and how to make it *related* to your audience. To take your presentations to a whole new level, you should also make them *original* and *enjoyable* – two further success criteria from the Five Principles for Powerful Presentations. Let's look at how to spice things up and add some colour.

If you have an important message you want to communicate, ask yourself, 'Is there a story I can tell to illustrate my point?' In the context of a business presentation, a story could be a personal anecdote about yourself or someone else, a real-life example, a case study or a tale about a client's success.

As an aside, when it comes to personal anecdotes, you may think that sharing personal stories contradicts with the lesson from Chapter 12 on making it about the audience, not yourself. There's a distinction though. If a personal story is there to reinforce a particular point which is relevant to the audience, then it works. If it doesn't make a relatable point, then it doesn't make sense to include it.

Most business presentations are made up of 99% facts and, if we're lucky, 1% story. That's the wrong way round. It's often better to flip it and spend more of your time sharing examples. In his book *Lend Me Your Ears: All you need to know about making speeches and presentations*,[41] Professor Max Atkinson describes a study he made of audience reactions to presentations. He positioned one camera on the speaker and the other on the audience. The study found that whenever a speaker used the phrase 'for example', it grabbed people's attention. They lifted their heads or eyes in anticipation of what was to come. Tell more stories. It's one of the most powerful ways to make your presentations more original and enjoyable.

Storytelling examples

Here are two examples where storytelling has helped some of the clients I've worked with. In each of them, people will remember the story *and* the message. Storytelling is not about telling a story for the sake of it. It's about telling a story to illustrate a particular point.

1. Nishita Dewan, Director at CollaborateHQ

The organisers of TEDxStroud invited Nishita to talk about 'The Magic of Unlikely Alliances'.[42] She approached me to help ensure she was prepared to give a fantastic presentation. She wanted to nudge everyone to form diverse collaborations and to harness the potential of diversity of thought.

Nishita chose to discuss an unlikely collaboration between Great Ormond Street Hospital (GOSH) and the Ferrari Formula 1 team. She referenced a story about a couple of doctors from GOSH sharing their frustrations at the high error rates when transferring critically ill infants from the operating theatre to the intensive care unit. As they were having lunch, they shifted their attention to a Formula 1 race on TV.

By pure serendipity, they observed the moment the Ferrari team completed a pit stop in under seven seconds. They observed the precision and teamwork from a team of pit crew technicians working together to optimise the car for the track, and in that moment they realised the uncanny similarity between the pit stop and their handover process.

The doctors and their team packed their bags and travelled to the Ferrari headquarters in Italy to learn more about this handover process. From this transfer of knowledge, the doctors designed a new handover protocol with more sophisticated procedures and better coordinated teamwork. As a result, they achieved a 20% improvement in patient safety, effectively saving children's lives.

2. Diana Hudson, Director of the social enterprise Creative Exchange UK

Not all stories have to be as in-depth as Nishita's. Sometimes, giving a quick example is all you need. You read about Diana Hudson when we talked about principle one, *Simple*. I worked with her to prepare a presentation on the topic of 'Circular Economy'. She felt the audience didn't have much knowledge on the subject, so she included two examples as an explanation. She said,

'MUD Jeans is a company which is doing something pretty interesting: renting jeans! As a client, you can pay a subscription to own a pair of jeans for some time and exchange them for a different pair as your needs or requirements change.

'Another great example is Food Float, a not-for-profit that's making fresh, local food more accessible to people in and around Dorking in the UK. They work with local food producers and sell their products within the community. This minimises costs, packaging and miles and puts money back into the community, which is at the heart of the circular economy. It's really cool to see how these companies are making a positive impact on the environment while also being innovative and creative in their approach.'

Diana's choice of Food Float was excellent because it was relevant both to her audience and her message. Her presentation was for an audience in Dorking. The choice of a local example meant something to her audience and helped to explain what the circular economy is.

Aim for the right mix of logic and emotion

As you prepare your next presentation, think about some of the most important points you want to get across and ask yourself what story you can tell to illustrate your points. If you only include information, facts and figures, they'll touch the logical part of the brain. When you tell a story, it touches the emotional part of the brain, which can be far more powerful.

A good presentation must stimulate a mix of logical and emotional responses, so you satisfy both areas of people's brains. The exact proportion of that mix will be different for each audience, which will have its own unique requirements. Think of your presentation as a seesaw. A seesaw is parallel to the ground only when nobody is using it. As soon as two kids start playing with it, the seesaw starts going up and down. A seesaw parallel to the ground is equivalent to a presentation with an equal mix of logic and emotion. Depending on the context, you may want to shift the balance either towards your logical arguments or towards your emotional arguments. What you never want to do is have a presentation that relies on logic alone.

LOGIC   EMOTION

15
The Persuasive Power
Of Analogies

John embarked on an unusual mission as a young
boy: to collect enough wine corks to build a boat.
Amassing enough corks took longer than he expected,
and over the years, it became something of a running
joke in his family.

Thirty years later, John revived the idea and started
seriously collecting corks from bars, restaurants and
even a cork company. During a job interview at The
White House, the president's chief speechwriter asked
John about the cork boat project that he'd mentioned
on the bottom of his CV. When John started to explain,
the chief speechwriter looked sceptical. John could
feel his dream job slipping away. On the spur of the
moment, he came up with an analogy. Building a cork

boat is a lot like writing a great speech. In both cases, a jumble of small words or corks won't do much on their own, but if you put them into the right order, they'll take you on an amazing journey.

The chief speechwriter got the analogy and John got the job. After leaving The White House at the end of the Clinton administration, John fulfilled his dream by building a 22-foot Viking sailing boat out of 165,321 corks and sailing it down Portugal's Douro River. The author of *Shortcut: How Analogies Reveal Connections, Spark Innovation and Sell Our Greatest Ideas*,[43] John Pollack shared this brilliant anecdote about how the analogy helped him land a job as one of President Bill Clinton's speechwriters when I interviewed him for the Ideas on Stage podcast.[44]

As we saw when we talked about the curse of knowledge in Chapter 5, the more we know about something, the easier it is to fall into the trap of making our ideas too complex and technical. It's something I see business leaders doing all the time. They assume that the audience will understand something just because they do.

This becomes even more of an issue when the topic is complex, technical or new to the audience. Under those circumstances, it becomes even more important to present your ideas in an original and enjoyable way. In this chapter, I'm going to explore the power of analogies to help you do that.

An analogy is a comparison between one thing and another – to clarify or explain something. Using analogies is a powerful way to help your audience understand an unfamiliar concept. By linking something they don't know with something they do, you create a connection for them. That's when learning happens. The best way to explain something new is to connect it to something the audience already knows. There are three reasons why analogies are super powerful:

1. After millions of years of evolution, our brain likes to **recognise patterns**. When we come across something unfamiliar, we're predisposed to looking at it through the lens of what we already know. That's why people always say a new type of food tastes a bit like something they've had before or a new band is similar to another band they've already heard.

2. Analogies **trigger emotions**. In the previous chapter, I talked about how stories trigger the emotional part of our brain and how you can use stories in presentations so you're not only addressing the audience's logical side. It's the same with analogies. They also trigger emotions and these are often more powerful than logic when trying to persuade people.

3. Analogies help you move **from abstract to concrete**. They help you bring your concepts to life. When you communicate an idea, the risk

is that it remains conceptual. If you connect your idea to something the audience already understands, you turn an abstract concept into something concrete. That makes it much easier to understand.

Steve Jobs once said: 'Creativity is just connecting things.'[45] When presenting, one of the best things you can do to make your messages *original* and *enjoyable* is to connect things. Learning, understanding and retention happen when you make connections.

Analogies used by clients

Below are some real examples of analogies our clients have used. For each example, I've included some information about the context, the idea the presenter wanted to communicate and the analogy they used to illustrate the idea.

Diversity and Inclusion and Rome's Metro Line C

- **Context:** Presentation on the topic of 'Diversity and Inclusion'.

- **Idea:** When we talk about Diversity and Inclusion, we make a lot of assumptions. But the truth is, unless we take the time to dig deeper and investigate the issues at hand, we'll never truly understand what's beneath the surface.

- **Analogy:** When I lived in Rome a few years ago, they were building the third Metro line (Line C). However, work would often stop because they kept uncovering old archaeological sites that needed to be preserved. They had to conduct an extensive investigation before they could continue. This is what needs to happen with Diversity and Inclusion. We need to investigate and understand the issues at a deeper level to really understand what's below the surface.

Supply chain and food diary

- **Context:** A company selling software for supply chain management.

- **Idea:** Our software makes the invisible visible. It gives you accurate data on the areas of your supply chain which are hard to see and hard to measure. This helps you understand where your organisation is doing well and where it needs improvement.

- **Analogy:** A friend of mine told a dietician a while ago, 'I know I'm overweight, but I can't see why. I'm not eating that much.' The dietician suggested that she start keeping a food diary. After keeping it for a few days, the food diary showed why she was overweight. She was eating too much. Often, we can't see things unless they're in front of us. The same happens with your supply chain. Our software is like a food diary for your supply chain. It helps you see what's going on behind the scenes and identify the areas that need improvement. Just like a food diary can help you understand what's causing your weight gain, our software makes the invisible visible and gives you accurate data on the hard-to-see and hard-to-measure aspects of your supply chain.

Anger and homelessness

- **Context:** TEDxBrighton, 'Can Anger be Good for you?' by Margaret Rose-Goddard.[46]

- **Idea:** Anger is a more useful feeling than sadness.

- **Analogy:** What often drives human behaviour is anger. Anger can be good for you, but it's important to distinguish anger from sadness. Sadness gets us stuck, whereas anger moves us forwards. If I see a homeless person on the street and feel sad about it, then nothing happens. If I feel angry, then I want to do something about it. I want to help that person. Action and change often happen because of someone feeling angry about something. Anger can be good for you, once you do the work to channel it for change.

The anchoring effect

When you share an analogy, there's a powerful effect at play. Once we hear an analogy, we think, 'If *that* is true, *this* must also be true.' If what the presenter said about Rome's Metro Line C is true, it must also be true that we need to go deeper to understand the issues around Diversity and Inclusion. If it's true that a food diary can have a big impact on an individual, it must also be true that their software can help my business spot supply chain issues.

Researchers call this the anchoring effect. Analogies make our arguments more believable. Once an analogy anchors itself in your audience, it's hard to remove it. A study[47] by Nobel Prize winner Daniel Kahneman and Amos Tversky asked people to estimate the percentage of African countries in the membership of the United Nations after spinning a roulette wheel. Once the ball settled on a number from zero to 100, the participants were asked whether the percentage of African nations in the UN was higher or lower than the number showing on the wheel. They also had to guess the actual percentage.

The roulette wheel had a big effect on people's estimates. When the ball landed on ten, the average guess was 25%. When the roulette wheel showed 65, the average guess went up to 45%. The participants weren't making their decisions on their own – they were affected by the 'anchor' of the roulette wheel. When following a presentation, an audience will also be drawn to the anchor of your analogies, ie how things are connected to other things. If they believe *that*, they'll also believe in your idea.

16
Conversation, Not Presentation

Have you ever driven your car when you were tired? You might have had that heavy feeling in your eyes and were desperate to close them and get some rest, but you couldn't. Let's say your partner was there with you but they were unable to drive because they'd had a few drinks or they were even more tired than you. It fell to you to be the nominated driver.

A good partner does everything they can to interact and help to keep you awake. They'll ask you questions, share anecdotes or select a great playlist on Spotify and sing along. It's the same in a presentation. A good presenter will do anything to keep the audience awake and engaged. There's nothing more boring than a one-way lecture which makes an audience feel like they're being talked at. Despite that, too many business leaders deliver presentations which are more like one-sided lectures. They believe their job is to speak for thirty minutes while others listen. These kinds of presentations, which don't consider the needs of the audience, are tedious and unsuccessful.

How do we do things differently? In this chapter, I'll explore how to bring the audience into your presentations and make them feel involved, which is another way to make your presentations *original* and *enjoyable*.

In her book *Presenting Virtually: Communicate and Connect with Online Audiences*,[48] Patti Sanchez says that a presentation should be a 'designed conversation'. A presentation should feel like a conversation. If you can manage to achieve that, then your presentations will be engaging and interactive. If the audience feels like they're helping to create the presentation with you, they'll want to listen and will feel more involved. An audience who sees that you're considering their needs, questions and priorities will feel more valued. It's *designed* conversation, not just conversation. This means that the conversational element of a presentation – the moments of interaction with the audience – are not left to chance. They're planned.

That's not to say you can't also have some spontaneous moments of interaction. If you see an opportunity to discuss something with the audience which wasn't planned, go for it! Confident presenters will always include moments of interaction with the audience and plan them ahead. You want to keep the audience's attention high. And the best way to do that is to interact with them from time to time.

How often should you interact with your audience?

A professor from Imperial College London decided to apply some science to boring presentations. Robert Ewers, who attends numerous academic conferences in his role as Professor of Ecology, wanted to establish whether dull presentations are actually longer, or just seem that way. To do that, he sat through fifty talks and timed them. Out of the fifty talks, he found thirty-four talks interesting and sixteen boring. He discovered that the thirty-four interesting talks lasted, on average, eleven minutes and forty-two seconds. The sixteen boring ones were, indeed, longer and went on for an average of thirteen minutes and twelve seconds. He also had supporting data showing that the longer the talks, the higher the chances of them being boring.[49]

What does this mean for you? To keep things simple, what it means is that the attention of your audience will decline after about ten minutes. It doesn't matter how interesting your subject is. Ten minutes are enough for most people. The ten-minute rule is wired into our physiology. If you can keep your presentations within ten minutes, you're doing your audience, and yourself, a big favour.

If your presentation is longer than ten minutes because you have a certain amount of material to get through then break it down further into ten-minute segments. In between each ten-minute chunk, find a way to maintain the audience's attention or to win it back. You need to interact with the audience every ten minutes.

What about online?

It's even harder to keep an audience engaged online. There are too many distractions for them and you don't have a direct connection. In a webinar, for example, some people will have their cameras off. Everyone has mastered the art of trying to look as though they're concentrating while secretly checking their emails, football scores or feeding their dog. So, the ten-minute rule becomes the three-minute rule online. You need to interact with your audience every three to five minutes.

For example, I worked with Nicola Askham, also known as 'The Data Governance Coach', to develop an online presentation for potential clients. The subject of her talk was 'The Six Principles for Successful Data Governance'. It was advice on how organisations can design and implement successful data governance frameworks.

We made sure we had a moment of interaction for many of her key points. I've summarised them below so you can see how we broke it down.

Message	Interaction
Introduction	Where are you joining today's presentation from? Let me know in the chat
Data governance can be challenging	What's your biggest challenge with implementing data governance right now?
View data as an asset	Do you believe that your organisation views data as an asset? Type Yes/No in the chat
A data governance initiative isn't a one-off project. It's a long-term journey	Is your organisation treating data governance as a one-off project? Type Yes/No in the chat
Have a clear vision of what you're trying to achieve	Are you clear on why your organisation is doing data governance? Type a number from 1 to 4 in the chat (1 = Not clear at all; 4 = 100% clear)
Tailor your data governance framework to the specific needs of your organisation. One-size-fits-all doesn't work	Have you tried to use a standard framework in the past?
If you want to be successful with data governance, keep it simple	On a scale from 1 to 5, how complicated is your data governance framework?

Note that she included seven moments of interaction. Her presentation was thirty minutes, so that was one moment of interaction every four minutes or so. Nicola designed these moments of interaction in advance. She knew she had to ask those questions. She practised the interactions when she rehearsed her presentation.

As you can see, it doesn't have to be complicated. As long as you involve the audience in the conversation, they'll appreciate it. Above all, make the audience do something (even if it's as simple as answering a question). When the audience does something, it means they're there with you. They're listening to you and paying attention to what you're saying, rather than feeding their dog.

Suggestions for interactions

Here are some suggestions of how you can build in some moments of interaction with your audience:

- Ask questions.
- Invite them to type their responses in the chat.
- Launch a poll.
- Use breakout rooms.
- Invite them to complete an exercise or a quick test connected to the material you've covered.
- Ask them to reflect on your ideas and share their thoughts with you or the person next to them.
- Ask them to share their key takeaways with you.

And finally, three tips for getting it right:

1. Make sure your interactions relate to your material or it can feel fake and forced. None

of Nicola's questions were for the sake of it. For example, when she asked the audience what their biggest challenge was, she was talking about the main challenges around data governance.

2. Keep it simple. You don't want questions that require a lot of thinking. This is especially true for online presentations when you want people to react quickly in a chat box. If you want to ask more detailed questions, it's best to direct people to a breakout room to brainstorm ideas. Sometimes a simple binary question (eg yes/no) is all you need.

3. Spread the moments of interaction equally throughout your presentation. If Nicola had dropped seven moments of interaction during the first ten minutes, it would have annoyed the audience and the last twenty minutes would have been boring.

When you come to plan your next presentation, after you've developed a clear storyline (which we looked at in Chapter 8), remember to work on some moments of interaction. The best approach is to look at your key messages and come up with some ways to involve the audience. How can you make the audience do something? Include those moments of interaction in your storyline. Write them down. It's a *designed* conversation. Remember to practise the moments of interaction when you rehearse or you'll forget to use them when you're in front of your audience.

Chapters 14 to 16: KEY IDEAS

- If you can bring your presentations to life with stories, they'll have more impact on your audience.

- Stories can be anything which provides a real-life context to your message. Think about what anecdotes, examples and case studies you can tell the audience which fit with your narrative.

- Analogies are also powerful, especially when communicating ideas which are complex, technical or new. An analogy is when you draw a comparison between one thing and another.

- They create what is known as the anchor effect. We hear an analogy and we think 'if *that* is true, *this* must also be true.'

- The best presentations feel more like conversations. Include moments of interaction every ten minutes or so. It's even harder to keep people engaged online, so aim to bring that down to every three or five minutes.

 One thing

It's time for you to capture what you've learnt again. What's the one thing you're taking away from this section? Write it in your notebook.

PART THREE
SCORE IN ACTION

We've now covered all of the Five Key Principles for Powerful Presentations: Simple, Clear, Original, Related and Enjoyable. In this final part of the book, I'm going to put everything together and give you a step-by-step guide on how you can apply our five principles in your next presentation. You'll also get some tips on how to design and deliver your presentation in a way that complements your message.

I've also included some content on public speaking nerves, authenticity and why there's never been a better time to master your presentation skills.

17
Putting Everything Together

If you've stuck with me this far, you should now be familiar with the five SCORE principles for powerful presentations. Now the question is, how can you apply these principles the next time you prepare a presentation? What process can you follow? In this chapter, I'm going to explain how to employ each of the principles in practice to develop a powerful message for your next speaking opportunity.

The preparation process

Here are the steps we go through at Ideas on Stage when we work with our clients.

1. Understand your audience

Start with the ABC of preparation. Ask yourself some questions about your *Audience*, their *Burning needs* and the *Context*. This will help you develop a presentation which is *related* to your audience.

2. Brainstorm your key messages

Take some time to brainstorm ideas that you can include in the content of your presentation. Think about your audience and your topic, and ask yourself:

- What do I want my audience to do after my presentation?

- What do they need to believe and/or feel to take those actions?

- What do they need to know?

Try to come up with more than one answer for each of these questions. Your answers will provide you with the top line key ideas to include in your presentation.

3. Bring it to life

The next step is to bring your ideas to life. Look back at the previous answers and invest some time in making each one as *original* and *enjoyable* as possible. Think about whether you have any stories, examples, anecdotes or analogies to include. Turn abstract ideas into concrete ones.

4. Simplify your message

Distil the core idea behind your presentation down to no more than seventy words. Make sure your message follows the 'What, So what, What next' format. This gives you three key benefits:

1. It helps you drill down to the *simple* core message you want your audience to understand and remember.

2. Asking yourself 'So what?' forces you to think about the audience and make your message about them. That's the key to great presenting.

3. Your 'What, So what, What next' will give you a great conclusion for your presentation.

5. Identify your three key messages

Once you've completed the brainstorming and simplified your single core idea, it's time to identify the three key messages that support your idea. You might just identify the three most important points from your brainstorming and disregard the rest. However, if your content needs to be more involved, look for patterns and connections. If some ideas can be linked to others, group them together into a key message.

Don't give yourself too much of a hard time over this process. You don't have to reinvent the wheel. You've already identified ideas in your brainstorming session. Just flesh them out and give them some structure.

6. Create a clear storyline

Your three key messages will give you the main body of your presentation. Now it's time to include some other elements to give the presentation a *clear* storyline. Here's a summary of my suggested structure:

- An opening that grabs the audience's attention.

- Three key messages.

- A brief recap to summarise your key idea.

- Next steps to give a specific call to action.

- A Q&A to answer questions from the audience.

- A conclusion (What, So what, What next).

7. Include moments of interaction

The icing on the top of your presentation is to include some moments of interaction with the audience. What questions can you ask them? How can you draw them into the conversation? Go back to your storyline and identify some opportunities at key points to interact with the audience.

Additional factors to consider

Follow these steps and you'll be able to consistently develop a compelling message. While your message is the most important factor for the success of any presentation, it's not the only one. There are an additional two steps to consider. Once you have a captivating message, you may also need to reinforce it with powerful visual aids, if appropriate. You also need to make sure you're ready to deliver your message with confidence in front of an audience, online or on stage. For this, the most important thing you can do is to rehearse.

In the next two chapters, I'm going to give you some tips on slide design and rehearsing so you can reinforce your message both with your visuals and with your delivery.

18
Simplifying Your Visuals

The best things in life are often the simplest. Some of the best meals I've ever eaten have been simple – just high-quality ingredients presented in an uncomplicated way. However, it can take a chef many years of training and experience to learn that lesson. The same is true in lots of other areas of life, not least art. For example, in 1945 Picasso created a series of eleven lithographs called 'The Bull'. The series shows a bull in different stages of abstraction. Picasso started with a realistic bull, including details like the snout and hooves. Then he went through a series of iterations, removing details each time. The final sketch is beautiful in its simplicity. Picasso stripped away everything but a few simple lines to represent what is unquestionably a bull. It's a bull in its most pure form, drawn by a visual genius. Picasso has removed the unnecessary. Less is more.[50]

Randy Nelson, a former Dean of Pixar University and member of the Faculty of Apple University, used this example as part of an internal course called 'Communicating at Apple'.[51] Minimalism is integral to Apple products and its whole corporate philosophy. They always try to capture the essence of an idea in products which are as simple and intuitive as possible. When Steve Jobs presented Apple's new remote control in 2005, he demonstrated that all the standard remote controls available at the time had more than forty buttons. Apple created a remote control with just six: to go back and forth, turn the volume up or down, play or pause and select the menu. That's it. It is simplicity put into practice. Like Picasso, they also went through a series of iterations and kept removing buttons to a point where only the essential ones were available.

What does this mean for you?

This idea of simplicity is not important only in product design, but also in presentation design. Designing by subtraction is key. The French writer Antoine de Saint-Exupéry said, 'Perfection is achieved, not when there is nothing more to add, but when there is nothing left to take away.'[52] Not only is simplicity in your designs more elegant – it also ensures that your slides don't compete with what you're saying.

Known as 'selective attention', research shows that the information we receive orally competes for our attention with the information we receive in written form,[53] so it's counterproductive to echo what you're saying in your slides. If you show a slide full of text, the audience will need to decide, 'Do I read the bullet points or do I listen to the presenter?' It's not possible to do both things at the same time. So, keep your slides simple. One idea per slide. There's no point creating slides full of bullet points which replicate what you're saying. Think about billboards. They rarely contain many words. The best billboards are just a big image and a few words. You can take the same approach and adapt it for your slides. Instead of using lots of words, show an image or an icon that illustrates your point, combine an image with a few words or show just a few words or a big number.

Another way to think about it is to apply the five-second rule. Every time you show a slide, make sure it's simple and intuitive enough for your audience to understand the message in no more than five seconds. Think of your slides as visual aids that support, reinforce and amplify your message. *You* are the presentation, not your slides.

When I talk about simplicity in design, I often get asked, 'What if I have to include more details?' Many presenters think that this approach doesn't apply to them. They insist that they need to do things their way, for their audience (who want to see more details on slides) or for their industry.

People tell me they need to have slides they can display during their live presentation and use as a handout afterwards. If you're one of those presenters, here's the solution for you: separate, separate, separate.

Confident presenters separate. What you say during a presentation (your words), what you show (your slides) and what you give (your handout) are three different things you should separate.

Confident presenters always keep their slides simple and visual. Slides and documents are different and you should use them for different purposes. If the audience requires more detail, have a handout prepared which you can distribute before, during or after the presentation (depending on the context). The handout includes all the information and details. The slides remain simple. Think about slides and documents as two separate tools for different purposes and pick the right tools for the job. You don't need a full set of fancy clubs to play a bit of crazy golf with your kids.

19
The Unexpected Value Of Rehearsing

Mark Leruste, CEO and founder of the Ministry of Purpose and host of the award-winning podcast 'The Unconventionalists', delivered a great TEDx talk in 2017. I interviewed Mark for the Ideas on Stage podcast and he shared the behind-the-scenes preparation which had gone into his talk.[54]

Mark told me how he had worked on the content for the talk for months, losing sleep and stressing about it at the same time as starting a family and founding a new business. With just three weeks to go before the big day he told himself, 'The only way I can make this talk good is if I test it.' Mark committed to testing the speech to twenty-one friends over twenty-one days in twenty-one different locations across London. He said it was one of his most challenging experiences as a speaker. Much of the feedback was awkward and difficult to hear, but also very useful.

With just a few days to go before stepping on stage in front of a live crowd, one friend admitted he felt the speech was 'boring'. Mark told the friend an alternative idea – that being an entrepreneur is much harder than most people are willing to open up about – and decided to scrap everything he had been working on for five months and start afresh. The result was a fantastic talk, 'What They Don't Tell You About Entrepreneurship',[55] which clocked up more than one million views and became the most watched TEDxCardiff talk to date.

It shows why rehearsing – especially in front of someone – is so important. Without that honest feedback from his friend, Mark would never have made such fundamental changes which ultimately made for a great experience for his audience.

When you watch the best athletes, their movement seems natural and effortless. Tennis champion Roger Federer appeared to glide around the court delivering perfect strokes in a relaxed fashion. The reason elite performers look so at ease is because of the years of dedicated practice they've all put in. No one is born with the ability to excel. It requires lots of hard work to get to the point where everything flows naturally.

The same is true for business presentations. It's impossible to deliver a great speech without rehearsing it. And yet, most business leaders fail to rehearse their presentations, certainly not to the level which is required. For some, rehearsing can feel like wasting time or silly. Let me be clear: rehearsing is mission critical in your ability to communicate your well-honed idea. You can spot a presenter who hasn't rehearsed. They fail to appear spontaneous or to deliver a presentation which flows in a smooth way. They use lots of verbal fillers – phrases like 'you know', 'like', 'actually', 'um', 'ah', 'er', etc. They fail to own their message, seem unprepared and sometimes panic before or during the presentation.

Rehearsing is the best way to improve your delivery

When you see a great speaker in action, it's easy to assume it comes naturally to them. However, just like the swan whose legs are pedalling furiously under the water's surface, exceptional speakers work hard to make it look natural. There's no great speaker who hasn't toiled on rehearsing in advance. Nothing great happens without effort.

The more you run through a presentation, the more freedom you'll have to look spontaneous and deliver your message with ease. Rehearsals will help you become a more confident presenter, focus on the audience, own your message and enjoy the moment. All those finer delivery skills like eye contact, body language and use of voice can only come if you rehearse.

Do you rehearse?

When I ask this question during my coaching and training sessions, most people tell me they do. When I probe deeper, it becomes clear that they don't understand what proper rehearsal is. Most diligent people who have an important presentation coming up will put effort into thinking about what to say. They'll go over the structure in their head. They might even flick through their deck, thinking about what to say for each slide. This is not rehearsing. This is valuable preparation which will help, but it's not enough to get you to the level you want.

Just like the final rehearsals for a West End show, rehearsing means delivering your presentation out loud as closely to the real situation as possible. It means speaking all the words from beginning to end without stopping and as if there's a real audience. The closer the rehearsal can be at simulating the environment or conditions you'll face, the better.

For example, for an online presentation, launch the conferencing software you'll use, share your screen, place your laptop at the right height and go through your material as if you're presenting to a real audience. If you plan to stand up for the real event, do so now. If it will be an in-person presentation to six people, place six chairs in front of you or stick six Post-it notes on the wall to practise eye contact with.

If you can rehearse in front of a mock audience of colleagues or friends, as Mark did, that's ideal. This creates more pressure compared to rehearsing on your own. The more pressure you can place yourself under during rehearsal, the better the real presentation will go. The well-known adage 'practice makes perfect' isn't entirely true. Practice only makes perfect if you do it well. Gareth Southgate understood this when he prepared the England football players for potential penalties at Euro 2020. The England manager, who had himself missed a penalty at Euro '96, put the players through rigorous penalty training routines in every practice session. The players had to recreate and repeat the moment they walk from the halfway line up to the penalty spot. Gareth also got them to practise fixating on the ball, picking a spot to aim for and sticking with their decisions.[56] Sadly, for England, it wasn't enough and they once again lost on penalties in the final, but their intention and preparation were excellent.

When we don't prepare, things almost always go wrong. Hollywood director Michael Bay was booked to appear at a Samsung event at the Consumer Electronics Show in 2014. Michael was supposed to answer some easy questions on stage about his work. However, he made a mistake by starting to answer a question that hadn't been asked yet. This messed up the flow of the autocue and the operator had no idea whether to move forwards or backwards. Without the comfort of the autocue, Michael fell apart. After fumbling through an attempt at winging it, all of a sudden, he left the stage and disappeared. He was unprepared and unable to deliver his message without assistance. His fight or flight response kicked in and he decided to get out of there.[57]

An important lesson from that incident is that it doesn't matter what your role is, how experienced you are or how much knowledge you have – when placed under stress, the body always wins. The adrenaline rush and the feelings we experience always win over our ability to remain calm and relaxed. Unless we rehearse. Michael Bay produced and directed films like *Armageddon*, *Pearl Harbor* and the *Transformers* film series. He's one of the most commercially successful directors in history, but even he couldn't counter the powerful forces which come with lack of preparation. The only way to ensure you can overcome those feelings and reactions is through rehearsal. The best way to conquer stage fright is to know what you're talking about. And the best way to know what you're talking about is to rehearse.

How many times should I rehearse?

There's no magic number as to how many times you should rehearse in preparation for a typical business presentation. What works for one person may not work for another. Based on my personal experience and from working with our clients, I can say that *three* times is the absolute *minimum*. For some people, that's enough. Others will benefit from further rehearsal. Many of my clients tell me they can only internalise their message if they rehearse about ten times.

The next time you have a presentation, rehearse three times at the very least, out loud and in conditions as close as possible to the ones you'll face on the day. It's also important to space out your rehearsals. Don't cram them all into the last minute. For example, if I had two weeks before an event, I would push myself to do five rehearsals equally spaced over that time. Hermann Ebbinghaus, a German psychologist who did pioneering research into memory, published a detailed study in his book *Memory: A Contribution to Experimental Psychology*.[58] He suggested that learning is more effective when we space out the sessions. We have a much better recall of information if we do that rather than cramming the study into one day. That advice applies just as much to rehearsing for a presentation as it does to revising for an exam.

I often hear business leaders worrying that rehearsing will make them appear robotic and over-prepared. The only time that will happen is if you haven't rehearsed enough. In his book *TED Talks: The Official TED Guide to Public Speaking*,[59] Chris Anderson uses a great analogy. He says that rehearsing is like climbing a mountain. If you start climbing a mountain, but stop straight away, you'll never get to the top. It's only when you reach the top that you can start coming down. If you only rehearse once or twice for a presentation and stop, you will appear robotic. You need to keep climbing to get to the summit and reach the point where you've *internalised* your message.

This is different from trying to memorise a presentation word for word. That works for some people, but in most cases it's not necessary. What's important is to internalise your content. You need to know exactly what to say, what the key messages are and what the structure is. That's when you'll be confident in your ability to deliver a great presentation. The more you rehearse, the more confident you'll be. Stop at the point you know the material well enough to be able to deliver it without any aids. Or stop at the point you can deliver your presentation while you're doing something else, like driving or doing household chores.

When I talk about the value of rehearsing, a common fear is that people don't have the time to rehearse. The issue here is getting your priorities right. Finding the time to rehearse will pay dividends. Often, when we feel we don't have the time, it's because we're focusing on the wrong things. Instead of spending extra time tweaking slides or worrying over every exact word, invest time into rehearsing. It will pay off. The concept of rehearsal is common to all performers – whether that's musicians before a concert, actors before a play or footballers before a match. As business presenters, why do we have the arrogance to think that we can do a great job even if we don't practise?

As sales speaker Lee Warren says, when you think about rehearsing, you only have two options: you either rehearse before a presentation or you rehearse in front of the audience.[60] In other words, if you haven't rehearsed in advance, your presentation will just be a rehearsal for what could have been.

20
Taking Control
Of Your Nerves

Alexandra Galviz has been named LinkedIn Top Voice UK twice. She's best known for blogging under the hashtag #AuthenticAlex. She is also the co-creator of #LinkedInLocal, the biggest hashtag campaign on LinkedIn that kicked off an offline community and scaled it in over 100 countries and 1,000 cities.

When I interviewed her for the Ideas on Stage podcast,[61] she told me that she was terrified of speaking in public at the start of her career. It was one aspect of her job which she hated the most. At some point, two different companies offered her two different jobs. One role didn't involve public speaking, but the other did. What did she do? She chose the one that required lots of public speaking on purpose so she would have to face her fears.

It's an important lesson. The worst thing you can do is shy away from public speaking just because you get nervous. Instead, you want to keep presenting *despite* the inevitable anxiety. That way, you'll learn to control and minimise the fear and become more and more comfortable with it. If you make the decision to keep presenting despite the nerves, you'll get to a point where you can control your nerves much more easily.

The reason why I'm sharing this story is because Alex isn't alone. Most people are afraid of public speaking. Research shows that about 75% of the population has some level of public speaking anxiety.[62] If you also feel nervous before a presentation, you're in good company. I'm a presentation coach and I feel nervous all the time before a presentation. It's common to feel nervous before speaking in public, even among accomplished presenters.

This can happen in many different contexts, not just when delivering a formal presentation to a large audience. It can be equally nerve-racking to address a few colleagues in a meeting or to wait your turn to introduce yourself at a networking event. Even children waiting to be called upon by the teacher to answer a question can find it intimidating. That feeling of anxiety can strike any time we know the spotlight will be on us. The symptoms might include sweating, increased heart rate, dry mouth, difficulty breathing and needing to urinate.

Sound familiar? The trouble is that in business, no matter what your role, you're likely to have to undertake some level of public speaking. Perhaps you need to pitch a new product to a potential client or you want to share your vision and strategy with your team. Maybe you're trying to raise funding for your startup. When you give your boss an update on that project you've been working on, you're speaking in public. Even when you just share your ideas during an internal meeting, it's public speaking.

If you can't control the anxiety and nerves in these situations, you'll miss out on important opportunities to win new clients, secure the backing of your team, seek investment, persuade your boss you're the right person to lead a project or increase your credibility at work.

Why do we get nervous?

That feeling of nervousness is all down to our natural fight or flight response. Our brains are hardwired to flee from a threat. Standing in front of many pairs of eyes all staring back at us can trigger the urge to run away.

Our brain doesn't always stop to consider whether those eyes are a tiger about to attack, or just an audience of like-minded conference attendees gazing at us while secretly wondering what's for lunch. It's all down to evolution. If you're alone in a remote area and you have a tiger in front of you (which our ancestors faced), adrenaline kicks in to make your heart pump faster. The biological aim is to get more oxygen to the blood and muscles, giving you the resources you need to fight the tiger or try to outrun it (good luck with that!). In that life-threatening situation, it's a useful response. However, we sometimes experience the same body response when we speak in public.

There's a film I love called *Chasing Mavericks*[63] about Jay Moriarty, a surfer from California who surfed one of the biggest waves in history. Big waves are known as 'mavericks'. He's practising holding his breath underwater with his coach, Frosty, when a shark appears above them. Jay panics and tries to shoot to the surface but Frosty stops him and, luckily, the shark doesn't spot them. Once they're back at the boat, Jay tells Frosty that he was afraid. 'You weren't afraid. You panicked,' Frosty replies. 'Fear is healthy. Panic is deadly.'

Those words had a profound effect on me. I hadn't ever thought about it that way before, distinguishing that fear and panic are two different emotions. I don't often encounter sharks (thankfully), but I'm afraid of spiders. I used to go straight into panic mode whenever I saw one. The film inspired me to reframe my fear of spiders and learn not to panic. I'm still afraid of them, but I'm able to deal with it (if I use my long-handled spider trap to catch them).

Practical tips to control your nerves

When you know you're afraid of something it's easier to control it, whether that is sharks, spiders or public speaking. The question is, how can you control your nerves? Instead of suggesting any 'woo woo' remedies, here are some practical tips to help you do that:

- Drink water before your presentation to avoid a dry mouth.

- Get your body moving beforehand. It's good to get out for a walk. Anxiety causes a lot of excess energy to flow through your body and you want to get that energy out. Movement is a great way to do so.

- Take a few deep breaths with your belly (not your chest). Breathe in through your nose for four seconds (feeling your belly rise); breathe out through your mouth for six seconds (feeling your belly flatten). It works better if you can make the breaths out longer than the breaths in. Chest breathing is what we do when we panic or when we're doing sport. If you want to relax, learn to breathe with your belly.

- Develop a quick warm-up routine which you can repeat before any important presentation. Try and put together a combination of breathing, muscle relaxation and vocal exercises. There's plenty of information available online about warm-up exercises. In Chapter 8, you met

Toby Trimble, the MD and founder of Trimble Productions. Before he presented at an important event, we did some warm-ups together. Toby said it was a game-changer as he felt far more relaxed and confident in his ability to deliver a great presentation.

- Interact with your audience straight away. Ask them a question or invite them to work on a quick exercise. You could ask them to reflect on an idea and share their answer with the person sitting next to them. This moves the attention away from you and buys you time to relax during those first few minutes. It also means that you create an enjoyable experience from the start by making your presentation more interactive.

These tips will all help to calm your nerves before a presentation. But they won't help you unless you rehearse. As we've seen in the previous chapter, the best way to reduce anxiety is to make sure you're rehearsed. Remember: the best way to control your nerves is to know what you're talking about – but don't be too hard on yourself. There will be ups and downs. Guy Kawasaki, one of Apple's early employees and a legendary marketeer, says it took him twenty years to get comfortable with public speaking. Now, he's world-renowned as a great presenter.

21
Don't Let 'Authenticity' Hold You Back

If we didn't eat with forks or use modern toilets (neither of which we used to do if we go far enough back), would that be a more authentic way of doing things? When learning the piano, would you resist your teacher's advice to sit up straight to play with more power because it didn't feel authentic? No. As with any other area of life, you would accept that you need to embrace new techniques to become better at the instrument. The changes might be hard, unnatural and uncomfortable, but you would do it.

Simon Sinek said that 'Authenticity is more than speaking. Authenticity is also about doing. Every decision we make says something about who we are.'[64] True authenticity is not about passively accepting who you are, it's about making proactive decisions to become better, while remaining true to yourself. There are many times in our day-to-day lives where we wouldn't choose to be authentic. It's the same with learning to be a better presenter. If you want to become a more credible, confident and convincing presenter, you need to worry less about authenticity and be willing to follow a new approach. Authenticity is a journey of constant growth towards becoming the best presenter you can possibly be.

Step out of your comfort zone

When I start working with clients to help them improve their presentation skills they often push back and resist change. As we've seen in the book, I encourage my clients to use a mix of logic and emotion, tell stories and include audience interactions. We also work on delivery skills like making eye contact and using gestures. A common concern is that the changes I suggest feel 'inauthentic'. People say things like, 'This is not me,' and, 'I don't want to act like someone I'm not.' It's a mistake to think that something which doesn't come naturally is somehow not authentic. When we're pushed outside our comfort zones, resisting change is a defence mechanism. Saying that it doesn't feel authentic is a way to get ourselves off the hook and to avoid having to do anything which is beyond our normal boundaries.

If you want to become a better presenter, there's no other way to do it. Positive change requires us to step outside our safe zone and that's hard to do. If you've ever resisted the idea of working on your presentation skills because of the authenticity dilemma, accept that implementing changes *is* authentic if you have the right underlying motives. The word 'authentic' is often used to describe works of art which are original. It's also used in restaurant contexts to mean that the food is a real version of what you would get in another country, for example, 'authentic Italian food' or 'authentic Mexican food'. Is it ever possible to be authentic in that sense? We all adopt and adapt recipes from other cultures. Loathe as I am to admit it, many people believe that Italian pasta probably came from China. In the same way, any art borrows from what came before. Of course, you want to be original and to be yourself. You don't want to be a copy of someone else. But 'you' is a work in progress. Work to become the best authentic version of yourself.

In *Act Like a Leader, Think Like a Leader,*[65] Herminia Ibarra coined the term 'authenticity paradox'. She describes the difficult choice between being yourself (doing what comes naturally to you) and doing what it takes to be effective. If you want to achieve results, it often requires doing things that don't come naturally. In the context of presentations, there are good reasons to strive beyond what feels comfortable. The aim is to persuade an audience to follow your call to action, so you can achieve your goals. If your motivation for working on your presentation skills is because you want to help the people you seek to serve, and reach your goals, then by making changes you are being authentic.

True authenticity has nothing to do with your behaviour. It's the motivation behind the behaviour. For example, if I pay you a compliment, it could be sincere, or I could be doing it out of courtesy. In other words, the same compliment could be authentic or inauthentic, depending on the motivation behind it. The same applies to any other behaviour – including your decision to take your presentation skills to a higher level.

Instead of thinking about authenticity, focus on being empathetic to your audience. Empathy is the key – the empathy to imagine what your audience would expect to hear, what their needs would be and what story would resonate with them.

Three ways to stay true to yourself

1. Think values, not feelings. Stop concerning yourself so much with how you *feel* and focus on what you *value*. The best presenters will include emotion in presentations, make eye contact and use hand movements which connect with their message. Doing any of that for the first time when you're not used to it can *feel* unnatural and uncomfortable, but you *value* your audience and *value* the results you'll see from a great presentation. Your behaviour, and your presentation style, should be driven by that. If you're having a conversation with a friend and you *feel* bored, you wouldn't interrupt, because you *value* the friendship. It's the same with an audience. Put their needs above yours.

2. Start with self-awareness. There's no authenticity without self-awareness. Take a good look at yourself and be honest about your strengths and weaknesses. You must build on your strengths and overcome your weaknesses to become the best authentic version of yourself. You'll have to work on areas that are uncomfortable and unnatural if you want to become more effective. Authenticity cannot be used as an excuse for not trying to get better.

3. Don't see yourself as 'static'. There's no static 'you'. We're constantly changing, learning and developing. You're not the same person you were five, ten or twenty years ago. In terms of your presentation skills, you'll have improved since you first stood in front of people to deliver a message. As you develop, you're still the same person. You're still authentic. You just have better presentation skills. Don't limit yourself to the 'authentic' person you used to be or you'll hold yourself back.

Tips on how to improve while remaining authentic

1. Learn from *many* great speakers

A great way to improve as a presenter is to observe other speakers and adopt their techniques into your own style. You can do this *and* remain authentic, especially if you learn from lots of speakers.

Soaking up the best techniques from others is not copying; it's learning from the best. You're not trying to be Steve Jobs or Oprah – nobody else can be those people – but you can borrow from their styles. The key is not to borrow from just one speaker. If you borrow from many speakers, you can take what you learn and change and tweak it to adjust it to your own needs. As the playwright Wilson Mizner is supposed to have said, 'Copying one author is plagiarism, but copying many is research.'[66]

2. Aim for unconscious competence

Your journey towards becoming the best presenter you can be will take you through four stages of competence: from 'unconscious incompetence' to 'unconscious competence'. Put another way, you'll go from being oblivious to how little you know, to being so good at it that you no longer think about it. Management trainer Martin M Broadwell described the model as 'the four levels of teaching' in 1969.[67] To get to 'unconscious competence', you must put in the hard work in the middle stages which are 'conscious incompetence', when you know you still have a way to go, and 'conscious competence', where you're getting better, but have to work hard at it.

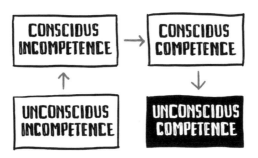

What stage do you think you are now? Maybe you're already at conscious competence, which is great. Or maybe conscious incompetence? It doesn't matter where you are. What's important is to recognise the stage you're at and put in the necessary work to achieve unconscious competence.

3. Do things that scare you

Every year I have fun hosting an event called 'Power-Point Karaoke'. We put selected speakers on the spot and ask them to improvise a presentation from a slide deck they've never seen before. It's hilarious for the audience, but daunting for the speakers. The event is an opportunity for even the most accomplished presenters to learn and grow. We had a woman come along to one event who told me that she wanted to do it because she had a personal challenge to push herself into doing things which scared her. I loved her motivation, accepted her application and she did a great job at the event.

If we want to get better at anything, sometimes we need to push ourselves into situations which are scary (rather than always going for what's easy, familiar and comfortable). The best way to grow as a presenter is by stretching your limits. This is how you grow from the presenter you are today to the presenter you want to become.

22
Why Now?

W arren Buffett, the billionaire investor and CEO of Berkshire Hathaway, is a firm believer in the value of public speaking for business leaders. His certificate from the Dale Carnegie public speaking course he took as a young investor still hangs on his office wall.

He tells business students that the one skill which will boost their value by 50% is public speaking.[68] Addressing a group of students at Columbia University in 2009, he said, 'Right now, I would pay $100,000 for 10 percent of the future earnings of any of you, so if you're interested, see me after class.' Having grabbed their attention, he added: 'Now, you can improve your value by 50 percent just by learning communication skills – public speaking. If that's the case, see me after class and I'll pay you $150,000.'

Public speaking is the most important skill you need right now. The main reason for any setbacks and disappointments in your business, role or career is a communication deficiency or lack of communication skills. If you can't convey your ideas to others, you won't be able to reach your true potential. For example, if your business isn't growing, there's a communication deficiency. If you're finding it hard to lead your team, there's a communication deficiency. If you're struggling to make a significant impact for causes you care about, there's a communication deficiency.

What are you going to do about it?

The most important step towards reaching your personal and professional goals and becoming the best version of yourself as a communicator can be summarised in three simple words: 'Do it now.'

This applies to anything in life, not least to public speaking. If you want to make change then you need to take action. Instead, most people who read this book will do nothing. They won't put the lessons into action or they'll put off doing anything to improve and procrastinate.

Procrastination (the action of delaying or postponing something) is the enemy of improvement. When we procrastinate, we're in a permanent state of wanting to do things but never actually doing them – we are passive spectators to the other people who are moving forwards. We come across procrastinators all the time. They say things like:

- I'd love to start a business, but now is not the right time. I'll wait for the perfect time.

- I'd like to travel to Southeast Asia one day, but now is not the right time. I'll wait for the perfect time.

- I'd love to learn how to play the guitar, but it doesn't fit in with my life right now. I'll do it next year.

- I need to improve my presentation skills, but it's not the main priority. I'll wait until things change.

The truth is, the perfect time will never arrive. There will never be a perfect time. Perfection is an unachievable ideal. Instead of focusing on *perfection*, think about making *progress*. My business mentor once asked me to create a brochure for a new product I was launching so I could use it during sales conversations with potential clients. It took me months to create one brochure. To me, it was never ready because it was never perfect. One day, after months of tweaking and changing and improving, I was so proud of myself that I texted him and said, 'My brochure is 99% done'. 'What a great accomplishment,' I thought. He replied with one sentence: '99% done is not done.' That was a huge lesson for me. Almost done is not done. Done is better than perfect. Now is better than later.

If you want to achieve your goals, you need to have a healthy sense of urgency. Don't fall into the trap of standing still when you could be doing something to improve. Top entrepreneurs and business leaders are implementers. They take action to move towards their goals. They make sure that what needs to be done gets done today, not tomorrow. If you've ever asked yourself, 'When is the right time to start working on my presentation skills?' the answer is *now*.

Mastering the art of public speaking can be rewarding. You'll be rewarded in your business and your career, but there will be no reward without action. In this context, good things don't come to those who wait! Be the best presenter you can be. Be the best version of yourself. Start your journey *now*.

Conclusion

You made it to the end of the book. Congratulations! I hope you enjoyed going on the journey with me and found the book helpful. I hope you've gained a good understanding of what it means to create powerful presentations. I hope you can see why the best presentations are so much more than just PowerPoint. Having the keys to pitch, present and communicate your ideas will unlock opportunities to inspire your audience, increase your influence and make a positive impact in the world. Now you need to put everything into action.

If you take only one message away from this book, it's this: *focus on the fundamentals*. If you want to continue your journey towards becoming a more confident presenter, forget PowerPoint. Forget technology.

Tools and technology evolve all the time and they'll continue to do so, but the art of communication won't change. People often ask me, 'What has changed in your field since you started working as a presentation coach?' My answer is always, 'Nothing.' It's the same old story. The tools have changed, but the fundamental principles have not. And they never will. Focus on the things that don't change.

Of course, make sure you can use the tools, but they're easy to learn. It's not how good you are with PowerPoint and Zoom that will make you stand out as a communicator. What will give you the edge as a leader is whether or not you master the fundamentals of communication.

Depending on who you listen to, human beings have been talking to each other as far back as two million years or as recently as 50,000 years. Either way, we've been speaking for a long time. Our ancestor leaders stood in front of a group to make 'presentations'. They had to influence their tribes and communicate ideas long before PowerPoint came along. The Greek philosopher Aristotle mapped out a theory of persuasion, a guide to public speaking, more than 2,000 years ago. His ideas are still used by great communicators today.

The world will continue to evolve, as it has since Aristotle's time. How could the Ancient Greeks have foreseen computers, satellites, digital photography or the internet? In our lifetimes we're likely to see increasing automation, use of artificial intelligence, driverless cars and delivery drones. There will always be new ideas. But now, more than ever, having a good idea isn't good enough. Your ideas are worthless unless you can communicate them. If you want to secure your dream job, ship products, shape brands or spark your team's imagination, you must be able to persuade and inspire people.

This is not something that a robot will do for you. This is not something that software can do for you. You still need to take responsibility for communicating your ideas in the most powerful way possible. In our technology-driven world, being able to present with confidence is a fundamental skill that will become more important, not less. Business success depends on your ability to persuade, inspire and influence others. The better you can convince others to act on your ideas, the more you'll achieve. Entrepreneurs need to convince clients to buy from them. Startup founders need to convince investors to back their ventures. Business leaders need to convince their teams to follow them and deliver on their plans.

By reading this book you've taken an important first step. Becoming a more confident presenter is in your hands. It will take time and effort, but there's a path. Implementing the fundamentals, the tips and the techniques in this book is a small investment which will reap the biggest rewards in your business and in your life. Being able to present your ideas with confidence is not a soft skill – it's a fundamental skill that will help you achieve your goals. In fact, it's the single most important skill you can master.

What next?

1. **Take the scorecard.** If you'd like to start or continue your journey towards becoming a more confident presenter, the best place to start is the Confident Presenter Scorecard. Discover the areas in which you perform well and the areas which you need to spend time developing. Visit www.ideasonstage.com/score.

2. **Attend my live web class.** Want to learn more about how you can inspire your audience and increase your influence through great presenting? Register today for my live web class at www.ideasonstage.com/uk/masterclass.

3. **Book me as a speaker.** If you run a group or event for entrepreneurs or business leaders and you'd like me to talk about business presentations, please send me an email at andrea.pacini@ideasonstage.com. I can cover any of the topics in this book, and much more.

Don't wait any longer. Find opportunities to speak. Prepare powerful presentations. Your confidence will soar, your audiences will thank you and your business and career will thrive. Remember: until you are a confident presenter, business will be hard. Until you are a confident presenter, your only job is to become one. There's never been a better time than now.

Notes

1   P Waknell, *Business Presentation Revolution: The Bold New Way to Inspire Action, Online or on Stage* (Rethink Press, 2021)

2   D Dent, Oversubscribed – Become a Key Person of Influence, Facebook (26 October 2022), www.facebook.com/groups/oversubscribed/posts/2861206437357310, accessed 13 April 2023

3   L Warren, *The Busy Person's Guide To Great Presenting: Become a compelling, confident presenter. Every time.* (Rethink Press, 2018)

4   N Lorincz, 'How Allbirds Went from a Small Startup to a Billion-dollar Sneaker Brand in 4 Years', OptiMonk (27 January 2023), www.optimonk.com/how-allbirds-went-from-a-small-startup-to-a-billion-dollar-sneaker-brand-in-4-years, accessed 05 April 2023

5   J Haden, '20 Years Ago, Jeff Bezos Said This 1 Thing Separates People Who Achieve Lasting Success From Those Who Don't', *Inc.* (6 November 2017), www.inc.com/jeff-haden/20-years-ago-jeff-bezos-said-this-1-thing-separates-people-who-achieve-lasting-success-from-those-who-dont.html, accessed 05 April 2023

6   C Heath & D Heath, *Made to Stick: Why some ideas take hold
      and others come unstuck* (Arrow, 2008)
7   OgilvyMuseum, 'Famous "Fish on a Bicycle" Guinness
      ad' (20 April 2010), https://youtu.be/JRMgMXA1xuc,
      accessed 05 April 2023
8   L McCarraher & J Gregory, *Bookbuilder: The definitive guide
      to writing the book to transform your business* (Rethink Press,
      2020)
9   C Gallo, 'When Presenting, Simple Is Always Best…
      Always', carminegallo.com (10 May 2018), www.
      carminegallo.com/presenting-simple-always-best-always,
      accessed 05 April 2023
10   M McConaughey, Greenlights (Crown, 2020)
11   Oscars, 'Matthew McConaughey winning Best Actor | 86th
      Oscars' (2014), https://youtu.be/wD2cVhC-63I, accessed
      04 April 2023
12   Darren's Music and TV Cave, 'BBC Three – Three Is The
      Magic Number – Advert' (7 September 2015), https://
      youtu.be/hIqFv7si9q8, accessed 05 April 2023
13   T Bella, '"Just Do It": The surprising and morbid origin
      story of Nike's slogan', *The Washington Post* (4 September
      2018), www.washingtonpost.com/news/morning-mix/
      wp/2018/09/04/from-lets-do-it-to-just-do-it-how-nike-
      adapted-gary-gilmores-last-words-before-execution/,
      accessed 05 April 2023
14   'i'm lovin' it Wordmark', McDonald's Corporate Website
      (23 October 2019), https://corporate.mcdonalds.com/
      corpmcd/our-stories/media-assets-library/media-article/
      i_m_lovin_it_wordmark.html, accessed 05 April 2023
15   'Every little helps', Tesco (no date), www.tesco.com/zones/
      every-little-helps, accessed 05 April 2023
16   'New TV advert urges public to stay at home to protect the
      NHS and save lives', Department of Health and Social Care
      (10 January 2021), www.gov.uk/government/news/new-
      tv-advert-urges-public-to-stay-at-home-to-protect-the-nhs-
      and-save-lives, accessed 05 April 2023
17   'New campaign to prevent spread of coronavirus indoors
      this winter', Department of Health and Social Care
      (9 September 2020), www.gov.uk/government/news/new-
      campaign-to-prevent-spread-of-coronavirus-indoors-this-
      winter, accessed 05 April 2023

18   'Liberté, Égalité, Fraternité', Élysée (no date), www.
      elysee.fr/la-presidence/liberte-egalite-fraternite, accessed
      05 April 2023
19   'Declaration of Independence: A Transcription', National
      Archives (no date), www.archives.gov/founding-docs/
      declaration-transcript, accessed 05 April 2023
20   'Full text of Tony Blair's speech on education', *The Guardian*
      (23 May 2001), www.theguardian.com/politics/2001/
      may/23/labour.tonyblair, accessed 14 March 2023
21   'See it. Say it. Sorted', British Transport Police (no date),
      www.btp.police.uk/police-forces/british-transport-police/
      areas/campaigns/see-it-say-it-sorted, accessed
      05 April 2023
22   KA Carlson & SB Shu, 'The rule of three: How the third
      event signals the emergence of a streak', Organizational
      Behavior and Human Decision Processes (2007), https://
      doi.org/10.1016/j.obhdp.2007.03.004
23   M Abrahams, 'Matt Abrahams: Tips and Techniques for
      More Confident and Compelling Presentations', Stanford
      Graduate School of Business (2 March 2015), www.gsb.
      stanford.edu/insights/matt-abrahams-tips-techniques-
      more-confident-compelling-presentations, accessed
      05 April 2023
24   Dr DA Sousa, *How the Brain Learns* (Corwin, 2011)
25   Plato, *The Republic,* translated by B Jowett, Project
      Gutenberg (1998, updated 2021), www.gutenberg.org/
      files/1497/1497-h/1497-h.htm, accessed 06 April 2023
26   DM Bunce, EA Flens & KY Neiles, 'How Long Can
      Students Pay Attention in Class? A Study of Student
      Attention Decline Using Clickers', Journal of Chemical
      Education (22 October 2010), https://doi.org/10.1021/
      ed100409p
27   Wikimedia Foundation annual report 2009–2010, https://
      upload.wikimedia.org/wikipedia/commons/9/9f/
      AR_web_all-spreads_24mar11_72_FINAL.pdf, accessed
      05 April 2023
28   MT Moe & MM Carter, *The Mission Corporation: How
      contemporary capitalism can change the world one business at a
      time* (Rethink Press, 2021)
29   T Ferriss, 'The Holy Grail: How to outsource the inbox and
      never check email again', The Tim Ferriss Show (21 January
      2008), https://tim.blog/2008/01/21/the-holy-grail-how-

to-outsource-the-inbox-and-never-check-email-again, accessed 05 April 2023

30   United Nations, 'Leonardo DiCaprio (UN Messenger of Peace) at the opening of Climate Summit 2014' (23 September 2014), https://youtu.be/vTyLSr_VCcg, accessed 05 April 2023

31   R Sethi, *I Will Teach You To Be Rich: No guilt, no excuses - just a 6-week programme that works* (Yellow Kite, 2020)

32   'Homer's "gift" to Marge – a bowling ball' (21 February 2017), https://youtu.be/NqrFpoxWqfU, accessed 05 April 2023

33   E Ledden, *The Presentation Book, 2/E: How to Create it, Shape it and Deliver it!* (Pearson Business, Second edition, 2017)

34   D Miller, *Building a StoryBrand: Clarify Your Message So Customers Will Listen* (HarperCollins Leadership, 2017)

35   M Adams, *Seven Stories Every Salesperson Must Tell* (Kona Press and Michael Hanrahan Publishing, 2018)

36   'Wealth Management Digitalization changes client advisory more than ever before', Deloitte (Issue 07/2017), www2.deloitte.com/content/dam/Deloitte/de/Documents/WM%20Digitalisierung.pdf, accessed 05 April 2023

37   N Duarte, *DataStory: Explain Data and Inspire Action Through Story* (Ideapress Publishing, 2019)

38   Nat Geo WILD, 'Blue Whales 101 | Nat Geo Wild' (27 August 2017), https://youtu.be/bgiPTUy2RqI, accessed 05 April 2023

39   'Drug Safety Update', MHRA (March 2018), https://assets.publishing.service.gov.uk/government/uploads/system/uploads/attachment_data/file/686884/DSU-March-18-PDF.pdf, accessed 05 March 2023

40   J Medina, *Brain Rules* (Pear Press, 2009)

41   M Atkinson, *Lend Me Your Ears: All you need to know about making speeches and presentations* (Vermilion, 2004)

42   N Dewan, 'The magic of unlikely alliances', TEDx Stroud (30 March 2021), https://youtu.be/ZFaBwPOjv8A, accessed 05 April 2023

43   J Pollack, *Shortcut: How Analogies Reveal Connections, Spark Innovation and Sell Our Greatest Ideas* (AVERY, 2015)

44   A Pacini, 'Episode 22: John Pollack on The Power of Analogy in Communication', The Ideas on Stage Podcast (16 June 2021), https://youtu.be/D1oBUMixJLk, accessed 05 April 2023

45 G Wolf, 'Steve Jobs: The Next Insanely Great Thing', *Wired* (1 February 1996), www.wired.com/1996/02/jobs-2, accessed 05 April 2023

46 M Rose-Goddard, 'Can Anger be Good for you?', TEDx Brighton (18 March 2020), https://youtu.be/LotC0ij-VFk, accessed 05 April 2023

47 G Gavetti & JW Rivkin, 'How Strategists Really Think: Tapping the Power of Analogy', *Harvard Business Review* (April 2005), https://hbr.org/2005/04/how-strategists-really-think-tapping-the-power-of-analogy, accessed 05 April 2023

48 P Sanchez, *Presenting Virtually: Communicate and Connect with Online Audiences* (Duarte Press, 2021)

49 RM Ewers, 'Do boring speakers really talk for longer?', Nature (26 September 2018), www.nature.com/articles/d41586-018-06817-z, accessed 05 April 2023

50 See www.museepicassoparis.fr/fr/collection-en-ligne#/artwork/160000000003556

51 G Winfrey, 'Why Apple Trains Employees to Work Like Picasso', *Inc.* (11 August 2014), www.inc.com/graham-winfrey/why-apple-trains-employees-to-work-like-picasso.html, accessed 05 April 2023

52 A de Saint-Exupéry, Wind, Sand, and Stars (Publisher unknown, 1939)

53 K Cherry, 'Selective attention: Definition, types, and examples', Explore Psychology (4 March 2023), www.explorepsychology.com/selective-attention, accessed 05 April 2023

54 A Pacini, 'The untold story behind Mark Leruste's TEDx talk', The Ideas on Stage Podcast (19 October 2020), https://youtu.be/s7Da3rGuLvM, accessed 05 April 2023

55 M Leruste, 'What they don't tell you about entrepreneurship', TEDx Cardiff (19 July 2017), https://youtu.be/f6nxcfbDfZo, accessed 05 April 2023

56 J Cross, 'England Players Recreating "Walk of Shame" in Training in Preparation For Germany', *Mirror* (27 June 2021), www.mirror.co.uk/sport/football/news/england-euro-2020-penalties-germany-24408573, accessed 05 April 2023

57 'Michael Bay quits Samsung's press conference', CNET (6 January 2014), https://youtu.be/R4rMy1iA268, accessed 05 April 2023

58   H Ebbinghaus, *Memory: A Contribution to Experimental Psychology* (Franklin Classics, 2018)

59   C Anderson, *TED Talks: The Official TED Guide to Public Speaking* (Hodder and Stoughton, 2016)

60   L Warren, '5 warning signs that your next presentation is heading for trouble', LinkedIn (28 November 2019), www.linkedin.com/pulse/5-warning-signs-your-next-presentation-heading-trouble-lee-warren, accessed 6 June 2023

61   A Pacini, 'Alexandra Galviz on Communicating Authentically', The Ideas on Stage Podcast (17 February 2021), https://youtu.be/aliy6xwkck4, accessed 05 April 2023

62   A Heeren, et al, 'Assessing public speaking fear with the short form of the Personal Report of Confidence as a Speaker scale: confirmatory factor analyses among a French-speaking community sample', *Neuropsychiatric Disease and Treatment* (2013), doi: 10.2147/NDT.S43097

63   *Chasing Mavericks* (2012). Directed by Curtis Hanson and Michael Apted. [Feature film]. United States: 20th Century Fox

64   S Sinek (@simonsinek), 'Authenticity is more than speaking…' (29 October 2021), https://twitter.com/simonsinek/status/1454096955911688206?lang=en, accessed 06 April 2023

65   H Ibarra, *Act Like a Leader, Think Like a Leader* (Harvard Business Review Press, 2015)

66   F Case, *Tales of a Wayward Inn* (Garden City Publishing Company, Incorporated, 1940), p248

67   MM Broadwell, 'Teaching for learning (XVI)', The Gospel Guardian, Vol 20, No 41 (20 February 1969), www.wordsfitlyspoken.org/gospel_guardian/v20/v20n41p1-3a.html, accessed 05 April 2023

68   C Gallo, 'Billionaire Warren Buffett Says This 1 Skill Will Boost Your Career Value by 50 Percent', *Inc.* (05 January 2017), www.inc.com/carmine-gallo/the-one-skill-warren-buffett-says-will-raise-your-value-by-50.html, accessed 05 April 2023

69   Walt Disney Studios (@DisneyStudios), 'Of all our inventions for mass communications…' (28 August 2013), https://twitter.com/DisneyStudios/status/372846848262021120?lang=en-GB, accessed 06 April 2023

Acknowledgements

All I can do is borrow. I don't have original ideas, those that seem to fall from the sky out of nowhere into the brain of creative thinkers. What I try to do is take great ideas and shape them in interesting ways. If I can do that, perhaps they become useful to somebody else. Thanks to all the experts who contributed to this book without even realising it.

The most important person to thank is my wife, Valentina. When I wanted to quit my comfortable corporate role to start a business – with all the fears and uncertainty that come with it – you were the one who gave me the strength to keep going. I would have never done it without your support.

I'm also grateful to my clients, especially the first ones at the beginning of my journey as a presentation coach. They paid me while I was learning. I will forever be grateful for their trust.

I owe a huge debt of gratitude to Phil Waknell and Pierre Morsa, who co-founded Ideas on Stage in 2010, for giving me the opportunity and responsibility to launch Ideas on Stage in the UK and for always backing my ideas. Special thanks to Michael Rickwood and Joe Ross at Ideas on Stage, who were the first ones to see what then became a fantastic partnership.

To my other colleagues at Ideas on Stage: Ricardo Bonis, Vanessa Querville, Edoardo Sala, Frédéric-Pascal Stein and Marine Bénard. Also, Rose Bloomfield who was an integral part of our team until 2022.

To my previous assistant, Eles, and my current one, Ron Jane. Without your support (and patience), I wouldn't be able to do all the things that I do.

To Sean Hamilton, who put my thoughts into words. Your work was the foundation of this book.

To my beta readers: Phil Waknell, Vanessa Querville, Grant Wright, Jessie Wölke, John Pollack and Charles McLachlan. Thank you for your time and commitment to this project. Your feedback, input and insights have transformed my ideas into a story worth reading.

To Grant Wright from The Visual Jam, who designed the illustrations in the book. As Walt Disney is supposed to have said, 'Of all our inventions for mass communication, pictures still speak the most universally understood language.'[69] Visuals matter.

To Daniel Priestley and the Dent team. Everything I know about business, I've learnt it from Dent. They are the ones who encouraged me to write a book. They are also the ones – together with my publisher – who showed me how to do it.

To the publishers and editors at Rethink Press. Special thanks to Lucy McCarraher, Joe Gregory, Eve Makepeace, Anke Ueberberg and Lisa Cooper who edited my writing and packaged my ideas into a book.

To my amazing clients who have agreed to be featured in this book so other business owners and leaders can benefit from their case studies and examples: Patrick Tyrance Jr, Tom Katté, Diana Hudson, Richard Mawer, Paul Spiers, Jessie and Sebastian Wölke, Alan Furely, Toby Trimble, Paul McCluskey, Circulor, Eileen Hutchinson, Ollie and Jack Farrer, Susanna Lawson, Nishita Dewan, Margaret Rose-Goddard and Nicola Askham.

Finally, thank *you* for caring enough about your own development or the development of your team to buy this book. Here's to your impact.

The Author

 Andrea Pacini is a presentation coach and Head of Ideas on Stage UK – a presentation design, coaching and training company that specialises in working with business owners, leaders and their teams who want to become more confident presenters.

With offices in London, Paris, Barcelona and Milan, since 2010 Ideas on Stage has worked with thousands of clients around the world, including companies like Microsoft, Lacoste, The World Bank and over 500 TEDx speakers. They have also been featured in the *Financial Times* and *Forbes*.

Andrea has helped hundreds of entrepreneurs, business leaders and TEDx speakers create, design and deliver successful presentations while helping them transform their presentation skills.

He has been featured on numerous industry blogs and podcasts and has delivered training sessions at The Wharton Club, Impact Hub, Rainmaking, General Assembly and The Institute of Directors. He is a mentor at Virgin StartUp, where he helps purpose-driven entrepreneurs launch, grow and scale their businesses through the power of great presenting.

Andrea is the main voice of the Ideas on Stage Podcast, where he has interviewed some of the most authoritative voices in the public speaking and leadership communication space, including Seth Godin, Garr Reynolds, Carmine Gallo and Dr John Medina.

Andrea is on a mission to stop great ideas from failing just because of the way they are presented. His vision is to help hundreds of thousands of business leaders share their message so they can grow their business, increase their influence, and make a positive impact in the world.

🌐 www.ideasonstage.com

in www.linkedin.com/in/apacini